The origin of the Faen ate

A rumi ous tale

Katie Withersby Lench

bridge books

The Origins of the Faenol Estate – a rumbustious tale
First published in Wales in 2010
by
BRIDGE BOOKS
61 Park Avenue
WREXHAM
LL12 7AW

© 2010 Katie Withersby Lench
© 2010 Design and typesetting, Bridge Books

Reprinted 2010

All Rights Reserved.
No part of this publication may be reproduced,
stored in a retrieval system, or transmitted
in any form or by any means, electronic,
mechanical, photocopying, recording or
otherwise, without the prior permission
of the Copyright holder.

A CIP entry for this book is available from the British Library

ISBN 978-1-84494-062-2

Printed and bound by
Blissett Group
London

This book is dedicated to
my parents and my husband, with love.

Contents

	Acknowledgements	7
	Author's Note	7
	Williams Family Pedigree	8
	Introduction	9
1	Thomas Williams	13
2	Sir William Williams, 1st Baronet	35
3	Sir Thomas Williams, 2nd Baronet	50
4	Sir William Williams, 3rd Baronet	59
5	Sir Griffith Williams, 4th Baronet	72
6	Sir William Williams, 6th Baronet	78
7	Ungentlemanly Behaviour	84
8	Quieter Times	93

Appendices

1	Faenol Inventory, 1669	107
2	Last Will & Testament of Thomas Williams, 1592	126
3	Last Will & Testament of Sir William Williams, 1625	131
4	Anwyl Manuscript	134
5	Last Will & Testament of Sir William Williams, 1658	135
6	Marriage Settlement of Margaret Jones & Sir William Williams of Vaynol, 1640	138
7	Marriage Settlement of Griffith & Penelope Williams, 1666	142
8	Last Will & Testament of Sir William Williams, 1695	148
9	Granting of the Vaynol Estate to John Gore, 1699	150

	Notes & References	153
	Index	158

Maps

1	Location of Faenol and other key places	12
2	Heart of the Faenol estate	33

Acknowledgements

Many, many people have helped to contribute to my understanding of the long history of the Faenol estate. My thanks go to all of them – you know who you are! I must also express my gratitude to the scholarly historians, most no longer with us, whose articles and books on the subject of north Wales in the Tudor and Stuart period have been invaluable.

My particular thanks go to Reg Chambers Jones and Roma Lort Jones, and to the unfailing helpfulness of the staff of Gwynedd Archives Service and Bangor University Archive.

Author's Note

For the sake of clarity, the modern spelling of Faenol has been used in all instances, apart from direct quotations where the spelling used by the original writer has been retained.

Maynol (Maenol) Bangor:
The medieval home manor of the bishopric of Bangor

Veynolgh, Veynelgh, Vaynoll, Vaynol, Vaenol, Y Faenol:
A sixteenth-century landed estate originally formed within the boundaries of Maynol Bangor.

Williams Family Pedigree

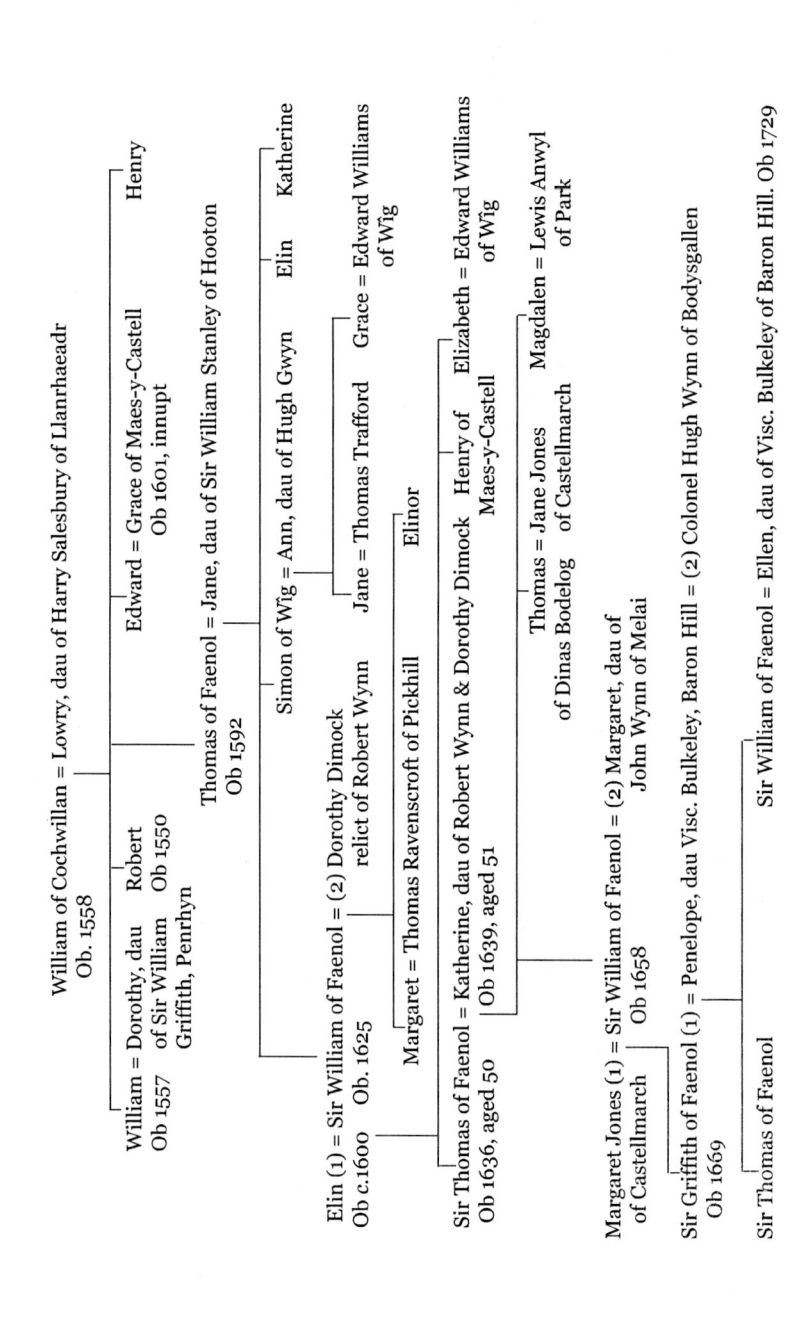

William of Cochwillan = Lowry, dau of Harry Salesbury of Llanrhaeadr
Ob. 1558

├── Robert Ob 1550
├── Edward = Grace of Maes-y-Castell Ob 1601, innupt
│   └── Henry
└── William = Dorothy, dau of Sir William Griffith, Penrhyn
    Ob 1557

Thomas of Faenol = Jane, dau of Sir William Stanley of Hooton
Ob 1592

- Simon of Wig = Ann, dau of Hugh Gwyn
- Jane = Thomas Trafford
    - Elinor
- Grace = Edward Williams of Wig
- Elin
- Katherine

Elin (1) = Sir William of Faenol = (2) Dorothy Dimock, relict of Robert Wynn
Ob c.1600   Ob. 1625

Margaret = Thomas Ravenscroft of Pickhill

Sir Thomas of Faenol = Katherine, dau of Robert Wynn & Dorothy Dimock
Ob 1636, aged 50   Ob 1639, aged 51

- Henry of Maes-y-Castell
- Elizabeth = Edward Williams of Wig
- Thomas = Jane Jones of Dinas Bodelog of Castellmarch
- Magdalen = Lewis Anwyl of Park

Margaret Jones (1) = Sir William of Faenol = (2) Margaret, dau of John Wynn of Melai
of Castellmarch   Ob 1658

Sir Griffith of Faenol (1) = Penelope, dau Visc. Bulkeley, Baron Hill = (2) Colonel Hugh Wynn of Bodysgallen
Ob 1669

Sir Thomas of Faenol

Sir William of Faenol = Ellen, dau of Visc. Bulkeley of Baron Hill. Ob 1729

Introduction

In the shadow of Snowdonia, hidden amongst the trees and gentle contours of an area of coastline south east of Bangor, is the heart of the once vast Faenol estate. People travelling from Bangor to Caernarfon know it by its high stone walls, and by the gates and gatehouses that signify exclusive access to the private world beyond. Ten years ago members of the general public had their first chance to venture through those gates en masse, as paying visitors to a music festival borne of a desire to bring world-famous singers and musicians to the area by local-born opera star, Bryn Terfel. Since then, thousands of people have become familiar with the parkland in its August bank holiday guise as a festival groundAs they wend their way back to their cars and coaches after the singing and the fireworks they are able to admire the backdrop of the late-Georgian mansion lit blue for the occasion.

The ground on which the unwitting festival goers tread silently records the vibrations of the well-heeled, expensively shod and stoutly booted – the latst in the centuries of owners, occupants, visitors and passers-by to visit. Voiceless, the land keeps its tales and secrets to itself, leaving people with varying views on the history of the Faenol estate; such views varying, dependent largely on how, or whether, their own lives or those of their forebears have been entwined with it. Some years ago, a lady with whom I was in conversation pondered that there could not be much history to research at the Faenol. Of course the truth is that there is more history lost to us at Faenol than we could ever know, but like all places it has a long story, and even the bones of it make a tale worth telling. This particular tale takes us back to the inception of the estate in the 1500s. But this date is by no means the beginning of the story of this valuable thousand-acre peninsula which bulges out into the Menai Strait, but it is a fascinating place to start.

It is a little-known fact that the origins of the Faenol estate are rooted firmly and indisputably in the upper echelons of ancient Welsh society. It is important to note this, as the more recent history, that of 300 years of English ownership and slate quarrying on an industrial scale, has long since eclipsed in popular memory that what came before.

The earlier history was born of the changing political, social and economic landscapes of the Tudor and Stuart periods. It is the story of six men, over six short generations, taking advantage of their freedom to acquire land, power and influence in the old county of Caernarfonshire. Businessmen, family men and men with good connections, the tale of the Williams family of Faenol is a fascinating insight into a Britain, and a Wales, where it was possible to buy into the landscape as a business venture, and not purely because you were in favour with a king or a prince.

Princely favour had been an advantage to an ancestor whom the Williams family shared with other Welsh gentlemen and with the Tudors themselves; the legendary figure of Ednyfed Fychan, seneschal to the Welsh medieval-prince Llywelyn Fawr. In addition to this illustrious ancestor, and of perhaps more practical value in the 1570s, the Williams family of Faenol were more recently and directly descended from the powerful houses of Penrhyn and Cochwillan which had held sway in north Wales since the late medieval period.

It took less than a century of making the right land deals and marrying the right girls for Faenol to become one of the premier estates in the county, coming through the English Civil War of the 1640s not only unscathed, but in better shape than ever before. Yet fifty years later the Faenol home of the Williams family would suddenly find its role as the flagship property of the estate eclipsed; business was conducted and decisions were made hundreds of miles away in the English homes of a series of new owners. As a symbol of a powerful landed force in Caernarfonshire, the house that we now call the Old

Hall slipped into anonymity as the home of employees rather than employers, and was destined to be overshadowed at the end of the eighteenth century by the building of the modern and prestigious villa which forms the nucleus of the large, white-stuccoed Faenol Hall that we know today.

Forgotten, but not gone, Faenol Old Hall was hidden behind screens of trees and walls; an unfashionable old house which was too close to the home farm for comfort, it was certainly not to be seen by the great and good, invited to enjoy the delights of the parkland and comforts of the new property. Little wonder then that the history imprinted on its old stone walls was equally forgotten. Few historians referred to it in their articles and books about Tudor and Stuart Caernarfonshire, except as a footnote. The industrial age and Faenol's involvement in roofing the nineteenth century's industrialising world has been, until now, considered far more noteworthy.

In the years spent researching the history of the Faenol estate, it became clear that its role in shaping the modern Caernarfonshire extended back to the sixteenth century, and that those formative years were every bit as important as those that came after. If you can picture the county as a stage, then the landed estates played the leading roles, with a cast of regular players who duelled on stage and fought in the wings, and who habitually proclaimed grand soliloquies of political allegiance. This is a story rife with skulduggery, deception, and violence; great feasting, romance and flattery. All the makings of a classic Shakespearian tale can be found in the annals of the great playwright's contemporaries here in north Wales, and for the first time, the story can now be told from the view of one of the county's least understood landed estates.

12 *The Origins of the Faenol Estate*

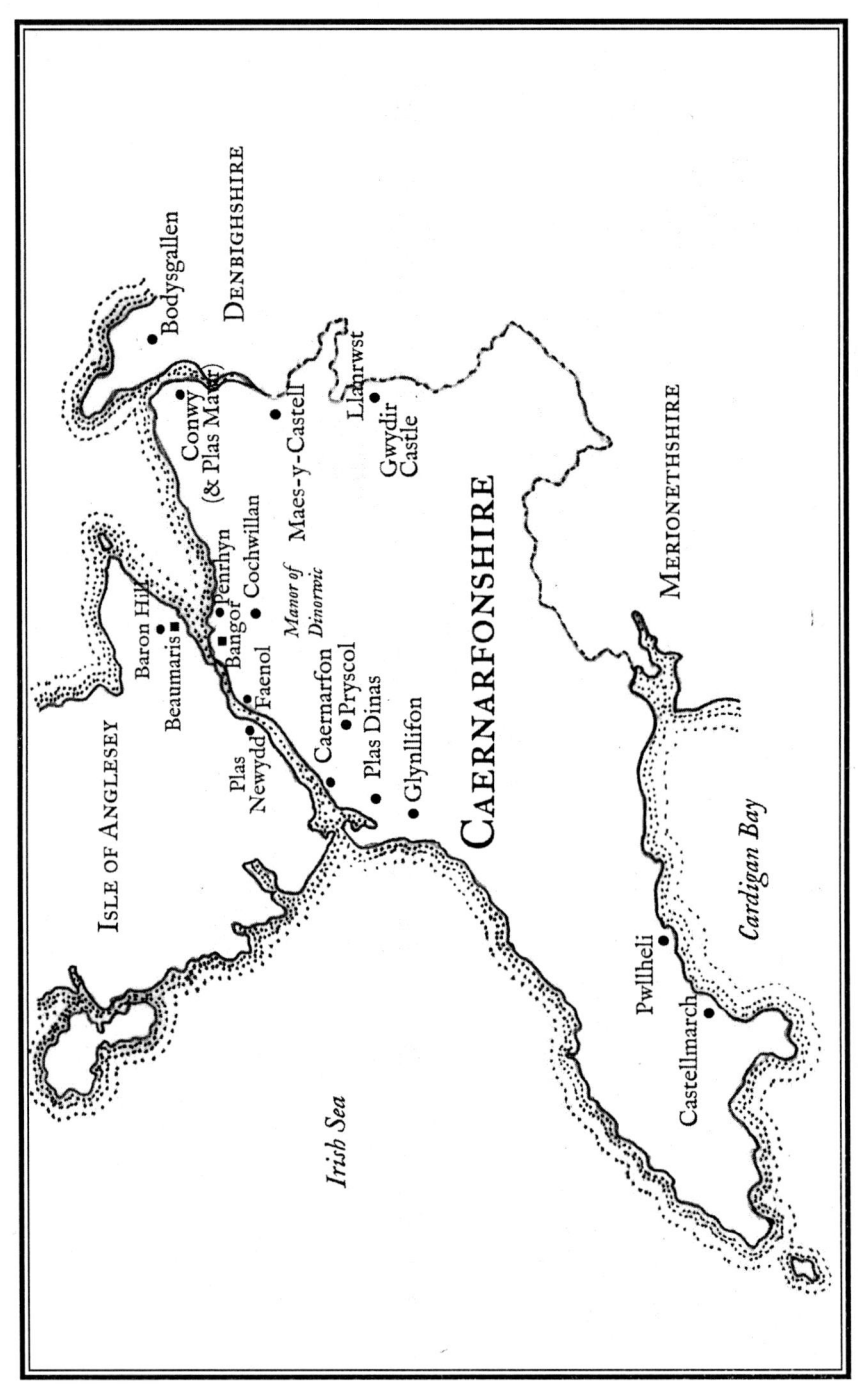

The location of Faenol and other key places on the county stage.

Chapter 1
Thomas Williams

In the period when Queen Elizabeth I succeeded to the throne and William Shakespeare was born, a young Welsh gentleman, Thomas Wyn ap Willim, looked with a keen eye to the future of his family line. The glories of his lineage drove him forward to a future that had by no means been assured by the vagaries of birth which placed him second in line behind his elder brother William. Strong and assertive by nature, Thomas listened to the stories and bardic songs celebrating the wonders and achievements of his Penrhyn forebears; why should he not desire to be a match to those men and women who presented such a formidable ancestry?

Even as a young man, Thomas' ambitions must have been clear in his own mind. He wasted no time setting about obtaining land and creating an estate, a business empire and powerbase. He was not in the least hindered by his brother, William's good fortune being the eldest surviving son which ensured that he would inherit the lion's share of their father's estate at Cochwillan, near Bangor.

Thomas' childhood followed the normal path for a boy from such a family. Although a school had been established in Bangor by the time Thomas was a young man, he, along with his siblings and probably his foster brother, Richard Morgan, was educated at Cochwillan by a tutor. This practice of fostering the child of a respected, but perhaps less wealthy, ancient family was an old tradition and could form life-long bonds. Indeed it was designed to do so. Certainly this was the case for Thomas Williams and Richard Morgan, for at the end of his life, Thomas ensured that Richard and his family were remembered in his will, securing their farm privileges and rent to the Faenol estate set at the rate for that year, 1592.

14 *The Origins of the Faenol Estate*

Cochwillan Hall, Tal-y-Bont, the childhood home of Thomas Williams.

From as early as the 1550s, Thomas had begun to seek power in the time honoured way, through the accrual of land. Even before he came of age, land was waiting in trust for him from the will of his childless uncle, Thomas Gethin. By the 1570s, he had established himself as a significant player in the stakes for land acquisition along with his contemporaries, the sons of the great landowners of the area. Many of these men who made up the gentry class of north-west Wales were so interrelated that the popular greeting of 'cozen' for relatives and friends would have been appropriate as well as fashionable. The relationships were complex; competitiveness, fights and marriages rocked the status quo backwards and forwards as the pull of land acquisition, prestige and power required alliances to be built up and wrenched apart.

Breaking with tradition, many of the young Welsh gentlemen of Thomas' generation styled themselves with a forename and surname in the English tradition. Thomas was no laggard in adopting some of these new traits, styling himself as 'Thomas Williams' on many legal documents throughout his life. For this generation the Act of Union was something in the past which had brought many advantages for the power-hungry Welsh gentleman. No longer was land automatically divided amongst the sons on the death of a father; the introduction of the law of primogeniture to Welsh landholding meant that one could leave the bulk of one's landed estate to one's eldest son. This made the rush for land, and the attendant power and prestige even more desirable. Now the heads of families were not just planning for their own lifetimes, they were establishing a great future for their dynasty, and creating personal immortality through a lifetime's work and achievements.

By the 1560s, Thomas was already a force to be reckoned with. So much so that he had successfully sought a fundamental building block of future landed greatness; a bride whose lineage was more solid, more extensive in reflected and conjoined influence even than his own. Preliminary dendrochronological findings at the time of publishing this book indicate that by the early 1560s he had completed his work on the Old Hall, creating a home of style and substance to which he could bring his bride home. That bride was Jane Stanley, daughter of Sir William Stanley of Hooton and granddaughter of Thomas' great friend Roland Stanley. These Stanleys were a substantial branch of the line of the earls of Derby whose landed influence included Lancashire and Cheshire as well as north Wales. Roland Stanley would never have allowed his eldest granddaughter to have married beneath *her*, or perhaps more appropriately *his* social status.

Sir William Stanley, Jane's father, was one of those characters from history who managed to follow his inclinations, in this case the cause of Catholicism, without (literally) losing his head. It is said that he had knowledge of the Babington Plot in the 1580s and that he was not always prudent in the way he spoke of Queen Elizabeth I. Although exonerated from having actual knowledge of the Gun Powder Plot, he found it necessary to ask James I for a pardon, and despite receiving one, was essentially exiled to the Low Countries where he died in 1630. However, at the time when he was looking for a husband for his daughter Jane, this was all in the future; in those days he cut a less controversial figure being retained in the service of his kinsman Edward Stanley, 3rd Earl of Derby. Although the Stanleys were brought up in the Catholic faith and Earl Stanley served as Lord High Chancellor and Privy Steward under the Catholic Queen Mary, they still found favour with Queen Elizabeth. Anyone who worked for the Earl, especially a kinsman like Sir William, found himself similarly favoured – until he stepped out of line.

For Thomas Williams, the outcome of his union with Jane Stanley, unless history hides something particularly undesirable about the woman herself, was a coup of considerable importance. If Jane herself favoured Catholicism it does not appear to have done either the relationship or Thomas' ambitions any harm, despite the fact that the ranks of Welsh gentlemen tended to conform under the Elizabethan Protestant Church. In Thomas' day there were small pockets of Catholicism and Puritanism in Wales, but there is no suggestion that the Williams family at Faenol were openly or habitually involved with the Catholic faith.

His marriage with Jane Stanley was a mirror through which we can reflect Thomas Williams' position in society, and she undoubtedly brought with her a significant dowry, which certainly included land as well as material goods. Women were a valuable bartering tool for liaisons from which both families could hope to gain. Certainly the Williams/ Stanley connection remained strong twenty years later when Thomas wrote warmly of his grandfather-in-law Roland Stanley in his will.

Locally, the 1560s was also a time when Williams and his contemporaries loosened the hold that one Hugh Bangor's family had on the land they had held for most of the sixteenth century. That land centred around Aberpwll and Farchwell, medieval townships now dominated by Faenol Park and adjacent to Y Felinheli. The century had seen considerable amounts of land sold off by the Bangor bishopric from within this, the bishoprical home manor – 'Maenol Bangor' (Bangor Manor). This land could then be sold to form the nucleus of a new landed estate.

Land was *the* important powerbase, but it was not the only means to money and authority. Trade, and an influence over that trade, was an essential part of Thomas William's portfolio and a list of people who had fishing rights on the Menai Strait in 1572 reveals that, along with other local gentlemen, he had inherited or acquired for himself one of these important rights. He may have fished for pleasure (and we would be right to visualise him as the sort of gentleman whose pastimes included hunting and coursing with hounds), but the significance of the fishing rights is one of control over the contents of the Strait, its shore and its associated earning potential. Control over other essential services was a landowner's privilege and as early as 1554 a document records the sale of land and a mill at Maes-y-Bont in Maenol Bangor to Thomas Williams, alias Thomas ap Williams ap William.[1]

Jane Stanley came to her union with Thomas Williams with no delusions about her role, or that of her husband. Marriage was a contract involving money, land and a place in society. What it offered for women obviously depended on the personality of their husband, but however girls may have dreamed of a chivalrous suitor they knew that suitability was the key to a successful marriage as far as potential parents-in-law were concerned. Their role in the marriage would be largely domestic, chiefly running the household, managing the household staff and providing heirs to the estate. Love was something of a bonus.

That Jane Stanley fulfilled her part of the bargain is testified by her brood of children. We know most about the sons William and Simon, through Thomas' will and through their activities as landowners, chronicled in the exchequer and local records. We know only about the daughters Elen and Katherine through their father's will. Elen had married Lewes ab Owen ap Meirick of Y Frondeg in Llangaffo on Anglesey, but by 1592, had been widowed with two of her own children and a clutch of her husband's from a previous marriage. Her father made provision in his will for any future marriage she might make, giving instruction that the estate should provide her with 500 marks, which equated to approximately £333 at that time, or around £42,000 in today's money. To her two young daughters he left £10 apiece towards their wedding dowries, which today we could think of in terms of over £1,000. The other daughter that he mentions is Katherine to whom he left our equivalent of £1,666 for her 'wife apparel', or the clothes she would need as a wife. We may presume by this that she was either already married to William Glynne of Plas Newydd (Glynllifon), or that her dowry had already been already paid out or allocated.[2] This was a gift therefore from a father to his daughter, and given that Katherine would be expected to demonstrate her rank by her outfits it is questionable how far this money would take her in the purchasing stakes. Products were far more labour intensive to make then than they are today and therefore cost relatively more to buy.

There is no record of Jane's age at the time of her death in 1579 but it is telling that there is no record or hint given of Thomas Williams remarrying. Had they married for love after all, or had love grown between them through the years? Perhaps Thomas for all his ruthless business mind could not contemplate remarrying, or perhaps no-one suitable presented themselves. It was then very unusual for a widow or widower not to remarry with haste, no matter what their personality, and yet there is no hint of a second wife in his will on his death twenty-one years later.

As ever, to support the role of a gentleman, it was important not just to possess land and business interests, but to be a significant and powerful figure in society and in the community. To achieve this Thomas spent a number of years in the role of Her Majesty's Crown Fermor in the manor of Dinorwic during the 1580s, a role which allowed him to collect the crown rents of the occupants of the land in this manor on behalf of the authorities. The significance of this post should not be underestimated, for the manor of Dinorwic was very large indeed and he would doubtless have made a tidy income from his position. Twenty years earlier he had merely leased land from the Crown in Dinorwic Manor in the township of Dinorwic. But, never one to sit idly by when an opportunity arose, when the time came to renew the lease on the land, Thomas Williams seized the chance to swindle his landholding neighbours in Dinorwic out of the rights to their land.

The story as extracted from the records tells how he offered to act on behalf of his neighbours in renewing the lease. Although these other families, like Thomas, were descended from ancient Welsh families and may have held their land for generations, he had no scruples about putting his ambitions before their heritage, and allowing Thomas to take their part in the negotiations was their undoing. Nervousness crept in as he and his henchmen arrived at their doors after dark bearing the new leases. When they protested that the paperwork was in English and that they were not able to read it, he dismissed their fears with the assurance that any inaccuracies could be sorted out at a later date. Eying the 'heavies' at the door they signed with justified misgivings. Their qualms were soon to come home to roost when they realised that the documents had given Thomas Williams the rights to the land which they and their ancestors had enjoyed for decades, if not centuries. Despite more than twenty years of litigation the other parties were never able to retrieve their land, although some of them were able to

Interior of Cochwillan Hall.

stay on their properties and land by paying large rents to Thomas Williams.[3]

This is not a pretty tale, but it was not an unusual story in Elizabethan Wales. In fact, the legal wranglings were prolonged by Thomas Williams' cousins, the Gruffydds from Plas Newydd on the opposite shore of the Menai Strait. These cousins, Maurice and Rowland, had wanted the Dinorwic land for themselves and encouraged the swindled neighbours to create trouble for Thomas. In 1587, he was obliged to take Maurice and Rowland to court, accusing them and others of the defacement of 'meers and boundaries' in Dinorwic township. In the next year he was recorded again in the court proceedings, this time accusing the powerful north Wales landowner, John Wynn of Gwydir, amongst others, of intrusion into his land in Dinorwic, and of diverting the course of a river flowing from the mountains into the 'Poole of Peris' and thereby depriving the tenants of Dinorwic township of water.

There is no doubt that it was a serious job trying to build up a landed estate at that time, no matter who you were. The sons of landed families were often sent to the Inns of Court in London to learn the legal trade, rather than be sent to university to extend their education. The intention was that a good knowledge of the law would be a fundamental strength in an estate owner, and doubtless it was. So crucial was the passing on of knowledge that elderly or ill fathers the length and breadth of Britain penned letters and journals full of their best advice for their sons, exhorting them to stay in control of finances, acquisitions and the activities of the men they employed to manage their estate affairs. Despite this, the history of the landed estate is peppered with tales of the 'bad egg', the son and heir who gambled away the family fortune or made an ill-advised investment in the commodities or marriage markets.

At the time when Thomas Williams was beginning his estate-building venture, Caernarfonshire and Anglesey were already dominated by a substantial number of long-established landed estates: the Bulkeleys of Beaumaris; the vast and powerful extended family of

Gwydir Castle, the powerbase of the influential Wynn family. [WAW]

the Wynns whose senior line was based at Gwydir in Dyffryn Conwy; Thomas' own relatives at Plas Newydd, Cochwillan and Penrhyn; the Glynns at Glynllifon and the Thomases of Coed Helen to name but a few. The fortunes of these landed estates would follow those of Faenol throughout the centuries, and in the sixteenth century they were in direct competition for any fresh land that came on the market with the men like Thomas Williams who were trying to establish themselves on the scene. Reading their letters to one another makes it clear that if you were not a good businessman you did not get on – there was no room for sentimentality.

Over the next hundred years, the Williams family would continue to build up their land and their influence in Caernarfonshire and Anglesey. Thomas Williams worked tirelessly to create a sound base for his successors to build on, and his efforts proved invaluable to them in the years to come.

The origins of Faenol Old Hall

There are signs that there may have been a building at Faenol before the Old Hall, as we know it, was created. It may even have been a gentleman's residence, although perhaps not a very large or significant one, as no known surviving documents make specific mention of a house on the site. The fourteenth-century Caernarfon court rolls make mention of a William de Haunton who had commissioned a cellar to be made at his house 'at Vaynol', but we must not get carried away in the belief that this was the same property; it may have referred to a property which was sited in Maenol Bangor, i.e. in the manor of the same name.

It is likely that Thomas Williams had his builders build upwards from the footings of an earlier building, as was common practice at the time. In this period, and in this area, it was possible that a gentry house might still be built with an open hall in the medieval style, but it is equally likely that the central core of the Old Hall with its upper floors and the heavy chamfered beamed ceiling of the ground floor hall represents Thomas' home as he requested it from his master builder

Roof timbers in Faenol Old Hall dating from the early 1560s. Now a bedroom, this was the 'Dyneing Room' in the seventeenth century.

Part of the front door frame at Faenol. The rose carved in the corner was undoubtedly a specific reference to the symbol of the Tudors.

in the early 1560s. In the 1560s provincial areas such as north Wales still saw houses built in the style of the long medieval shape, but the fashion for the open hall which Thomas would have grown up with at Cochwillan was definitely on the wane.

The Old Hall as it stands today represents at least four major phases of building work. The long roof-line running behind the two left-hand bays (when looking at the front of the property) represents the length of the original part – that is to say Thomas Williams' house. Initial findings suggest that the roof timbers of this part of the house were felled in the period 1558–62 and this in turn suggests a likely roof

Close-up of the hand-carved border frieze, Faenol Old Hall, seventeenth-century oak wall panelling. Now in the ground floor room, this was originally part of the upper floor oak panelling in William Williams's 'dyneing room'.

The wide oak boards, up to 30 cms wide, forming part of the ground floor at Faenol Old Hall.

construction date of the early to mid 1560s when we know that Thomas Williams was preparing to marry and to demonstrate his weight as a landowner. It follows therefore that we can accept with reasonable confidence that the floors were built on his instruction, and if so then we must also allow him to have commissioned the substantial oak-framed ceiling in the hall. This ceiling too harks back to an earlier period, a typical sixteenth century version of the heavily decorated timber-framed ceilings that had been the preserve of wealthy medieval nobles, and had filtered across the land and down through the ranks of the gentry as the fifteenth and sixteenth centuries progressed. The main chimney for this room, with its stack projecting out on the exterior wall of the house as a status symbol, just as it is at Cochwillan Hall, and as it appears to have been in the first phases of two Anglesey properties of Plas Coch and Plas Penmynydd, both also constructed around the time that Thomas Williams was establishing himself at Faenol. By the time Thomas was an old man this style of ceiling and exterior chimney were becoming quickly out-moded, even in rustic and rural outposts of Britain such as north Wales. Other features too became old fashioned as the sixteenth century entered its final decade and Thomas' life drew to a close. Like the gentry homes throughout the area, Faenol Old Hall

26 The Origins of the Faenol Estate

Faenol Old Hall, the north front.

would see some major building work during the next thirty years or so.

It would be impossible to tell the story of a place like Faenol and its occupants in the sixteenth and seventeenth centuries without considering religion to be a factor which was so much more influential in the every day lives of the majority of Britons then than it is today. When Queen Elizabeth I came to the throne she had recognised the importance of ensuring that her subjects were loyal to her both as the monarch and as the head of the Anglican Church, and eventually this was confirmed in law by the Act of Supremacy of 1559. This meant, amongst other things, that ordinary people were obliged to attend church services every Sunday. Such a thing would create uproar if Parliament tried to impose a law like that today, but the historian Geraint Jenkins, writing about the following century, tells us that nine out of ten Welsh people believed that the established church was 'the sole vessel of salvation'.[4] We can assume that the one out of ten who did not subscribe to an Anglican heaven probably considered Catholicism or some other form of Protestantism to be the route to the salvation of the soul. The point to consider is that the overwhelming majority of the population believed that they had a soul to save or damn and that religion per se was not a matter for opting in or out of, but a fact of life like the seasons or the weather.

Reading the wills of Thomas Williams and his sons, it becomes clear how influential a place the church had in society – not only for the purposes of worship, but as a part of the very fabric of life. Geraint Jenkins writes that 'the local parish church was the hub of village life, around which a host of social activities revolved. The rites and traditions of the church were bound up with the daily lives of parishioners.'[5] It would not be long before politics and religion would tear the country apart in a civil war. But even in peace time our protagonists recognised not only the importance of the church but the need to be seen to be recognising it, and they were remembering their duty to their community, to their souls and their role in supporting the official religion of the day when they wrote their wills.

Thomas Williams' will took the usual form in the preamble to his

Llandegai Parish Church.

bequests, dealing with the niceties of looking after one's soul, charming one's monarch and seeing to the fabric of the churches in his locality. He writes,

> In the name of God amen. The twentie nineth daie of Aprill in the yeare of our lorde God a thousand five hundrethe ninetie twoe in the thirtie fourth year of the reigne of our Sovereigne Ladie Elizabeth by the grace of God Queene of England, Ffrance and Ireland, defender of the faith. I Thomas Willim otherwise called Thomas Win ap Willim of the parish of Bangor in the countie of Carnarvon being weake in bodie but of whole and perfecte memorie doe make my testamente contayninge thearin my laste will in manner and forme followinge. Ffirste I commende my soule to the memorie of the lorde God Almightie my creator and redeemer…

Of course this was a standard form for the introduction to one's will, but there is no doubt that it covers the writer's back from all angles! Yet we should not forget that theirs was a much more genuinely devout age than ours and Thomas' bequests for repairs to the cathedral at Bangor and the churches of the parishes of Llandeiniolen, Llandegai and Llanberis come from a man who habitually attended church services throughout the area depending where he was residing at the time. His will later makes clear that he had at least two usual residences; his room at an unknown residence in Bangor as well as his house at Faenol. Llandegai was presumably the parish church with which he had become familiar as a child, being the nearest to Cochwillan Hall. There may also have been other places within Dinorwic Manor where he customarily stayed and attended church – the roads in the sixteenth century were notoriously bad and it was usual for people who had to travel around any area of Britain to seek accommodation with friends and family, or at inns, rather than risk their and their horses' necks by travelling back at night, or travelling backwards and forwards from home to an area if business dealings kept them in a locality for a while.

St Mary's Chapel at Faenol
It was with this in mind that Thomas made provision for worship at Faenol. In the winter or even in a wet summer, impassable roads could make a trip to a parish church or the cathedral out of the question. In addition, to have one's own chapel was a status symbol when most ordinary gentry devoted simply a room in the house to their private services and prayers. It is extremely rare in north Wales to find a surviving sixteenth-century private chapel such as this, which was not built as an integral part of the house.[6]

The St Mary Chapel at Faenol was built as a separate building, adjacent to, but not adjoining, the Old Hall. It is likely that it was built by Thomas Williams as part of the hub of his 'empire'. The surviving original stone mullions of the chapel match those in the surviving original windows of the house, although the stained glass in the chapel windows was replaced as part of the twentieth-century interior redesign by Sir Charles Assheton Smith. From a historical point of view, it is unfortunate that the original interior of this chapel has not

St Mary's Chapel at Faenol Old Hall.

survived. The larger and later seventeenth-century chapel at Gwydir Uchaf in Dyffryn Conwy, with its wonderful Italian baroque-inspired painted ceiling, reflects a later era and the influences on Sir Richard Wynn of high Anglican and Catholic friends and an interest in Continental affairs. A further decorated chapel (now lost) at Llandgadwaladr on Anglesey shows that north-west Wales certainly had a part to play in the seventeenth-century tradition of decorated ceilings.[7] No clues come down to us through history about the interior of the Faenol Chapel – no eighteenth-century traveller records any painted splendours and a newspaper cutting from the late nineteenth-century, describing its then role as a museum of stuffed animals, gives no hint of former finery. However, this does not mean that the chapel was likely to have been unadorned – there is no reason not to suppose that the beams at least were painted, if not decorated. After all, Thomas Williams had gone to the extra expense of creating a separate chapel, why would he not adorn the interior in the manner of the day?

When Thomas Williams of Faenol died in 1592, his four children upheld his will to be interred in the new family tomb at Bangor Cathedral with their mother Jane. Thomas' standing in the community was such that he was able to secure a family burial vault beneath the floor of Bangor Cathedral, placed prominently in the transept between the nave and the choir. To mark the spot an altar tomb was commissioned, carved with Thomas and Jane's names and the Stanley and Williams coats of arms. When a gentleman traveller, Mr Browne Willis, visited the Cathedral in 1721 the tomb was still there and he describes it for the readers of his 'Survey of the Cathedral Church of Bangor' as a

Tomb or Altar Monument, with a black Marble [Top] without any Inscription... On the Fore-part or South-side of it there seems to have been a Design to have Arms cut, but no such Thing was done, or if it was, they are since eras'd; but it has these short Inscriptions on one Side;

The surviving Faenol tomb panels, now displayed in Bangor Cathedral

> *Thomas Williams obiit* [died] May 27 1592.
> *Jana ejus Uxor,*[8] *obiit* May 25, 1579.
> At the End next the Quire is a Chev'ron between three Bucks Heads with a Crescent for Difference.

The diarist Edmund Hyde Hall also made note of this tomb on his visit in 1809, however it has since been dismantled and is now displayed on the walls of the south-west corner of the cathedral. The 'fine slab of black marble' that Hyde Hall speaks of has since disappeared.[9]

In this will, Thomas made good provision for his children, his foster brother and his trusted servants. One particularly favoured member of staff rejoiced in the provision of a lifetime's free rent and *meate and drinke for as long as he is contente to come for it* plus forty shillings on top of it. It is bequests such as these that really bring the man to life – here was a servant who had been loyal, given faithful service and become someone Thomas could rely on. Behind the words is a real bond between two living, breathing men – men who saw good and festive times, lean and bad periods, and, given the prevailing weather of the era, wet times and cold times too.

In a practical sense, the will is a statement of what remained of the Thomas' property, land and possessions after the lion's share had been apportioned to his eldest son William. Although it is frustrating to the historian that wills did not detail the land, goods and chattels to which the eldest son was to be entitled, it is obvious from what Thomas left to Simon his younger son, that the older brother William's share would have been considerable.

The Heart of the Faenol Estate

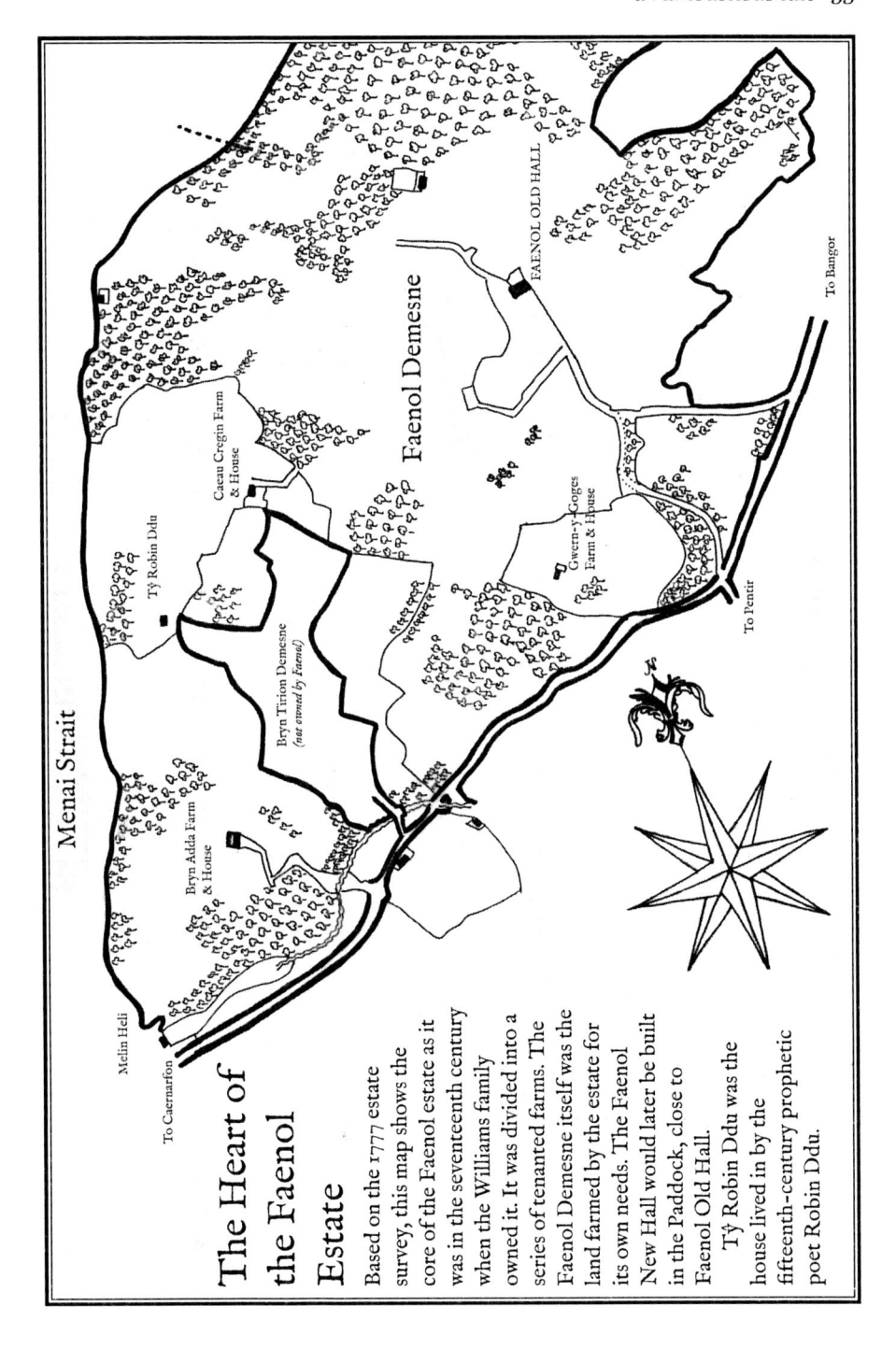

Based on the 1777 estate survey, this map shows the core of the Faenol estate as it was in the seventeenth century when the Williams family owned it. It was divided into a series of tenanted farms. The Faenol Demesne itself was the land farmed by the estate for its own needs. The Faenol New Hall would later be built in the Paddock, close to Faenol Old Hall.

Tŷ Robin Ddu was the house lived in by the fifteenth-century prophetic poet Robin Ddu.

– a rumbustious tale

34 *The Origins of the Faenol Estate*

The north front at Faenol Old Hall showing the stepped gabling on the right-hand bay

Chapter 2
Sir William Williams, 1st Baronet

Inheritance is usually considered in terms of tangible material goods or land and property. Yet William Williams also inherited a reputation and a position within the hierarchy of the local landed gentry and aristocracy. He also had a reputation within his own lineage to live up to and it appears that he was more than equal to the task. Taking on his father's mantle as Crown Fermor for the Manor of Dinorwic and as a prominent litigator, William continued to expand both the Faenol estate and the house at Faenol, or *Vaynoll* as it was known then. This expansion might be wondered at, given that a long period of poor weather saw harvest after harvest fail, causing great suffering and inflation throughout Britain for decades. That Caernarfonshire tenants suffered as much as any cannot be in doubt; in the 1620s the state of the local economy forced William's hand into agreeing reductions in rents for estate tenants and farmers in particular. However, he continued to acquire land to enlarge both the estate and his income which, as with most sixteenth and seventeenth century landed estates, came predominantly from the profits of its agricultural holdings. That William was able to continue to spend money in a manner befitting an estate owner even in such hard times, is testament to the already substantial nature of the Faenol rent books.

Like any successful businessman, William did not put all his futures into one sector of the economy. As later records show, Faenol owned, or was involved in, other businesses and properties throughout the area. However, although slate was quarried in Caernarfonshire in a small way during the Tudor and Stuart periods, it was on nothing like the scale of the quarrying of the nineteenth-century; this was not then the source of the estate's vast wealth. Nevertheless, in some areas the land had the propensity to yield more sources of income than just farming, and in the early 1620s a whole group of landowners were challenged in court over their right to quarry for millstones and 'slatestones' on their land; one of these men was William Williams of Faenol. Around a century earlier Hugh Bangor had been taken to task for digging millstones on the land that would later become part of William Williams' estate. Such men were part of a long history of Caernarfonshire landowners who found a use or a profitable market for the geology beneath their feet.

One use of the local stone was for extending or rebuilding their own properties. There are no records to show exactly when changes were made to Faenol Old Hall at this time, so it is hard to tell on which owner's instructions each modification and extension were made. A historian must use architectural clues such as window styles to puzzle out the different parts of the building. It is likely though that the right-hand bay (featuring a 'stepped' gable) on the front was commissioned by William Williams, whose second wife, Dorothy, was the widow of Robert Wynn of Plas Mawr in the town of Conwy.[10] The design of Plas Mawr makes substantial use of what is known as 'stepped gabling' and it is possible that the association with Plas Mawr in both this and the succeeding generation influenced the design of this extension to the front of Faenol Old Hall. Alterations and expansion of your main dwelling tells your friends and enemies that you have money, or credit, to spend on such a luxury, particularly if that change makes it ever more fashionable. Perhaps we should not see it as a luxury, for in the dog-eat-dog world of Caernarfonshire society one could not afford to be seen to be letting one's position, or perceived position, slip. In addition, William had a very good practical reason for needing to expand the Old Hall after his second marriage. Once both households were under one roof at Faenol, William and Dorothy between them needed initially to accommodate a total of twelve children of varying ages from their previous marriages.

As a young man, William Williams had agreed to take the hand of Elin Williams, his cousin's daughter from Cochwillan, in marriage.

Stepped gabling at Plas Mawr, Conwy.

Little is known about Elin apart from the fact that the couple were married long enough to produce possibly as many as five children. Their eldest son, Thomas, was born in 1586 and ten years later the couple commissioned a porch for the St Mary Chapel, which they endorsed with a stone marking the year and their initials. Again, these are real people with their lives marked out like ours by memorable occasions, both happy and sad, and perhaps the chapel porch represents one of these? A marriage, a christening, anniversary or a memorial; each would be suitably marked by an improvement to the family's private place of worship.

Some time between 1598 and 1605 William married for the second time to Dorothy Wynn (née Dimock). Neither can have had long to grieve for their previous spouses, William for Elin and Dorothy for Robert Wynn. During their

The 1596 date stone above the porch to St Mary's Chapel

The date stone over the main door to the Great Barn at Faenol bearing the date 1605 and the initials of William and Dorothy Williams.

marriage of over twenty years, Dorothy bore William two children, Margaret and Elinor, to add to the large number of offspring they already had between them from their first marriages. The new family bond was strengthened by the marriage of William's eldest son and heir, Thomas, and Dorothy's eldest daughter, Katherine, some time before 1611. The family was further unified by a long drawn-out courtroom battle, which they fought with the executors of Robert Wynn's will, over the inheritance owed to Dorothy's children from her marriage to Wynn.

Dorothy had managed the business affairs of her late husband through his final years of illness and seems to have been a very capable and determined woman. She was probably a good match for her new husband in personality and prestige, and she may have brought a substantial land and financial settlement to the union, for in 1605 William and Dorothy put their initials to a date stone on a substantial new stone barn at the Faenol Home Farm. Of the barns that survive today in Caernarfonshire from this period, the Great Barn at Faenol is the largest. No doubt at the time it was equally impressive and almost certainly a celebration of some kind was in order at the beginning of this building project. Perhaps the new barn replaced a previous timber barn of equally impressive proportions or conceivably it was a new building representing the expansion of the home farm along with the rest of the Faenol assets.

Farmers in today's Caernarfonshire would have little need for

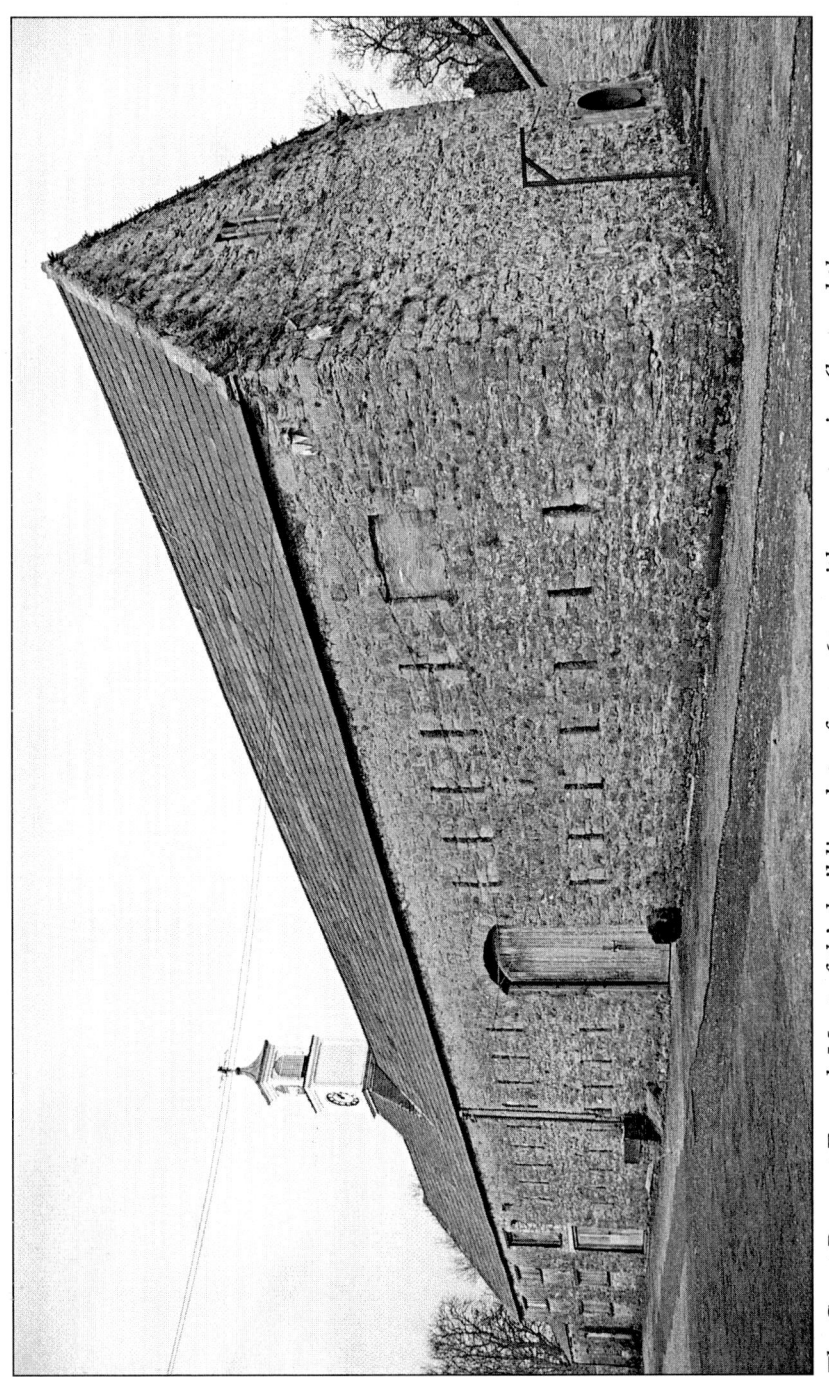

The Great Barn at Faenol. Most of this building dates from 1605, with an extension (beyond the nineteenth century clock tower) being added in the 1660s.

storing and processing grain on such a massive scale. We now live in a largely pastoral community where sheep and cattle graze in the fields or on hay mown and stored as silage. The residents of the area today have plenty of choice of food to buy at a variety of convenient locations; food which is imported into the county from other parts of the United Kingdom and abroad on a daily basis, using a transport network which was undreamed of four-hundred years ago. Their forebears were, of necessity, mixed arable and pastoral farmers, or small holders living a hand to mouth existence on what they could grow or raise and the little they could afford to buy to supplement it. In the seventeenth-century, they grew what was needed to survive in the area in which they lived; luxuries were imported in by sea only for those who could afford them. A grain barn was a functional necessity. Even so, a barn of this size demonstrates very effectively the physical dominance of Faenol in the landscape. Not only would the farm manager have stored and processed Faenol Farm's own grain crops in this building, but very often a landowner would have required his tenants to pay part of their rent in crops or livestock, just as they did in tithes to the church. Sir John Wynn of Gwydir in Dyffryn Conwy expected a percentage of his rents in this way and what was good for Gwydir was surely good enough for Faenol!

After his father's death, William Williams furthered his own cause, and also that of what we can now think of unequivocally as the Faenol estate, in the government of the region, holding positions of both high sheriff of the county and justice of the peace. Although he was considered a significant landowner and a power in the community by this point, he still worked to extend his estate. At the end of the first decade of the seventeenth-century, he was fortunate to be named as one of the beneficiaries from his uncle Edward Williams' will.[11] (Edward Williams of Maes-y-Castell, Dyffryn Conwy). Having inherited land around Maes-y-Castell and his uncle's house there, William continued to accrue land in this area, clashing with other landowners such as Sir Richard Bulkeley of Baron Hill, Beaumaris, over the rights to various portions of land on a number of occasions.[12]

Two antique prints showing Maes-y-Castell as it would have looked in the seventeenth century. [Elwyn Williams]

The 1582 date stone above the door at Maes-y-Castell, bearing the initials of Edward and Grace Williams.

One particular set piece of litigation lasted for six years where the two men wrangled over the right and title to Rhos-y-Vengill, Penrhyn Rhos and Rhos Einion in Penfro.[13] Historians often comment that litigation was the landowners' favourite indoor pastime, but we have to wonder if they had any concerns for the tenants of the property and land in dispute who could be dragged into something unpleasant against their will. At Penfro there were accusations of forcible entry, which if true, could have been both frightening and divisive. If two landowners were quarrelling over the land you farmed or the house in which you lived then to whom did you pay your rents? Whoever shouted the loudest or the one who sent round the most threatening agents? Tenants had everything to lose and little to gain in this situation.

It was every estate owner's duty to ensure that their family landholdings and assets grew or at least remained stable with each generation. Fathers had to provide for the future, hoping upon hope that at least one son would survive to inherit his legacy and if, as William Williams had, you had more than one son ('an heir and a spare' as the saying goes) you also had to plan for the inheritance of your other children. This land in the Conwy area was ultimately destined for William's second son Henry, but was in later times reabsorbed back into the Faenol estate. Much of the information about this period of Faenol's history comes from the records of other local landed estates with which the Williams family intermarried. This information comes from the manuscripts of the Baron Hill estate and the compiler of the catalogue of these papers suggests that William probably made Henry tenant of the freehold at Maes-y-Castell straightaway – certainly his younger son was thereafter known as Henry Williams of Maes-y-Castell and remained so until his death in 1658.[14]

The religious tensions in England and Wales between those following the old faith, and the majority who stepped in line with Anglicanism continued during this period. In coastal areas such as Caernarfonshire, there was constant fear that a Catholic enemy in the form of Spaniards would invade from a sympathetic Ireland just across the sea. This could only increase tensions and in 1620 the Faenol name came up sharply against them. In essence it sounds like trouble instigated from the Wynn camp at Gwydir, with whom tensions were perennially high.

After the Gunpowder Plot, a new oath of allegiance to the Crown and the official religion had been decreed. In 1620 an allegation was made by Sir John Bodvel, son-in-law of Sir John Wynn of Gwydir, and the Bishop of Bangor that Dorothy, Lady Williams of Faenol had been allowed by the Dean Edmund Griffith and a fellow magistrate to swear to a modified version of the oath – with the implication that her allegiances to the Crown and the official religion were not without some reservations. Such was the fear of Catholic invasion and sympathisers that this hint of dissention caused 'fowle disorder, tumult and ryott' which were only quelled when the advisers to the Crown, the Privy Council, questioned the two magistrates and getting to the bottom of the matter revealed that Dorothy had later taken the correct oath.[15] 'Fowle disorder, tumult and ryott' is such an evocative phrase and it does not take much to imagine the provocative rumours spread by those wishing to fuel or fan the tale of recusancy in their midst. Even with only basic methods of communication, it took little to light the tinder of fear until a tale took on a life of its own. Whether Dorothy was or was not following the old faith would have become of little matter as the spectre of Catholicism, and all that it seemed to embrace or engender in those volatile times, loomed over the community.

Despite this hullabaloo, in general, William's star suffered no more set backs than any of those of his contemporaries and the trouble surrounding Dorothy's oath did not appear to cause him insurmountable problems. In fact, only two years later, the Faenol estate had grown to the point where it was worth enough to allow William to purchase a baronetcy from King James I. The title of baronet was a new one, above the level of knight and below baron, created by James I to raise money for Irish wars and was available to landowners whose estate was worth more than £1,000. Accordingly, on 15 June 1622, William became Sir William Williams, Baronet, a title that his direct heirs would continue to inherit for a further five generations. Sir William was only the second Caernarfonshire man, and the fourth north Walian, to be in possession of such a title and that he could afford to spend such large amounts of money implies that the Faenol estate's rental income from land and property must have been enough to cushion him against the financial problems that agriculture was experiencing at this time. We see him in the Baron Hill papers busily buying, swapping and dealing in land in Dyffryn Conwy in the 1620s and although these are snapshots of his business dealings, there is no reason to presume that he was not doing exactly the same thing all over Caernarfonshire and Anglesey where we know he also had land.[16]

At their home at Faenol, William and Dorothy had not been idle in displaying their wealth, commissioning oak panelling and a substantial carved oak chimney-piece for the first floor dining room where they would have entertained the great and the good of the county. A very old photograph of this room shows that the highly decorative chimney-breast featured their heraldic arms in the centre, divided into four quarters each of which show the arms of the families with whom the Williams of Faenol were intimately connected through marriage and or lineage. The central point of this heraldic device was the Red Hand of Ulster, the emblem of a baronet. In the 1600s, it continued to be very important for a gentleman to demonstrate his connections, and this was especially so in Wales. Gentlemen were not averse to falsifying a

Arms of the Williams family once displayed on the seventeenth-century chimney breast at Faenol Old Hall. [Roma Lort Jones]

lineage if they felt theirs was lacking, but Sir William had a genuine ancestry to be proud of and was not shy of advertising his own success along with it.

The arms that he inherited through the Williams side of the family shows the heads of three men which came down to him from Ednyfed Fychan, the senior adviser to the medieval prince of Wales, Llywelyn Fawr and his son, Dafydd ap Llywelyn. History has it that these arms were granted to Fychan by the prince after he cut off the heads of three Englishmen slain in a battle against Ranulf, Earl of Chester. Interestingly, Sir William did not choose for the master carver to portray the Englishmen's heads in a medieval style on his dining room chimney breast, but in the style of King James I and the fashionable gentlemen of his own generation, with long curly hair and pointed beards. It would not be unreasonable to suggest that it might have been a fair representation of Sir William himself, self-aggrandisement being an acceptable attribute in European gentry circles; something which we can see very readily in the art of the early modern period where Italian nobles paid to be portrayed by renaissance artists at the scene of some momentous biblical or classical event.

The room was further resplendent with a great Turkish ('Turkie') carpet, sconces on the walls and seating around the tables for twenty eight! Such things are often lost to the winds of time, but one thing that we might have hoped to still be in situ, the carved chimney-piece, disappeared from Faenol Old Hall during the twentieth century. The panelling that adorned the walls around it still survives however,

46 The Origins of the Faenol Estate

having been moved downstairs to the front room once known as the hall. In order to make it fit its new location, the panelling was cut to size and, in its new position, disguised a disused door between the hall and the large room behind it that was probably Sir William's parlour.

A house of this great age has seen many changes of both status of occupants and the way in which the house was used. This parlour was added either by William or his father Thomas as an extension to the core of the house. Instead of having wattle and daub internal walls as would have been usual, there is a stone wall between the main hall and this parlour room which clearly indicates that it was once part of the exterior shell of the house. The addition of a parlour really brought the house up to date, reflecting the increasing desire of gentlemen for privacy in their homes, and the placing of the chimney and large stone fireplace at the far end of the room is typical of the style of properties in this area at the end of the sixteenth-century.[17] The centuries have left us with only one clue to the décor of this room – a small area of plaster applied directly to the stone work suggests that the walls of this room

Facing: Faenol Old Hall, east facade.
Below: The parlour at Faenol furnished in period style for the S4c programme Y Stafell Ddirgel *in 2001.*

The bedroom at Faenol furnished in period style for the S4c programme Y Stafell Ddirgel *in 2001.*

were fashionably plastered white in the manner recreated here in the same room by a film company.

Above the parlour must have been what we would call the master bedroom, but what William would have called a chamber. Here again there was a substantial fireplace because ladies and gentlemen of this period did not just sleep in their chambers, but used them as additional, more private reception rooms, as a place to have a quiet supper, or to read or write letters. Alongside the bed the room would have been furnished with a table and chairs, perhaps a side table and certainly a commode or 'close stool'. Off the chamber was a closet – not a wardrobe, but an even more private space where the master of the house might study or pray without being disturbed. Close friends or associates might be received in the chamber, while less intimate visitors would be shown into the parlour if their status warranted a more personal setting than the main hall, just inside the front door. Sir William, in his role as a justice of the peace, is recorded as having dealt with minor miscreants in his home rather than troubling the court with them when it was in session. They, like the travelling salesmen or tenants who would have come knocking at the door, would have made it no further than over the doorstep into the multi-functional hall room, a room panelled like the 'Dyneing Room' above, but more simply done. So, in addition to visits by friends and neighbours, William Williams would have expected people of all different parts of society to cross his threshold in some capacity or another, from petty thieves to his own tenants and estate officials.

In a rural area, a visit to a house like Faenol would be an undertaking made on foot, horse or even carriage and even from Caernarfon or Bangor would take a goodly amount out of the day. The household staff would be expected to produce refreshments for welcome and these would have been prepared by the cook, a man of some importance, in the new kitchen below the parlour, with its large arched fireplace containing a grate and ovens. Prior to the new parlour wing being built, it may have been that the kitchen was separate to the house in the medieval arrangement that minimised the risk to the house of fire.

After all their hard work, Dame Dorothy only got to enjoy her title for two years before she died in 1624 and shortly after, in the May of 1625, Sir William being ill and feeling that death may shortly be upon him, made haste to write his will. At his death that year, his baronetcy was passed on to his heir, Thomas, the eldest son borne by his first wife Elin.

Chapter 3
Sir Thomas Williams, 2nd Baronet

Sir Thomas Williams seems to have been another man of resolute ambition, if his actions during his life are anything to judge by. He had already promised his eldest sister Elizabeth money for her dowry if she was to marry after their father's death, and in his will Sir William had referred her to Thomas for 'further augmentation of her marriage porcon [portion]' hoping that Thomas would '(out of his natural love and affection towards her) treat her kindly and lovenigly'. Eventually, and we must hope that she did not feel herself to be 'on the shelf', he found her a suitable husband in their relative Edward Williams of Wîg, near Abergwyngregyn. Although some sisters and step-sisters were either already married, dead or provided for in his father's will, Thomas' household at Faenol had three unmarried sisters and half sisters to care for, as well as the three children Katherine had borne him since their marriage in or around 1610. There was no doubt that the estate could provide a suitable income for Thomas' family in appropriate style and, before Thomas died in 1636, further extensions were made to Faenol Old Hall, adding another room at each level and a wide oak staircase leading off a central hallway.

Less is known about his land dealings than those of his father, although we do know that he continued to pursue and be pursued by Sir Roger Mostyn through the courts on the subject of Mostyn's dealings regarding Robert Wynn's will and the money due to Sir Thomas's step-brothers and sisters. Undoubtedly he was interested in the financial situation of his step-siblings (including of course Katherine his wife), but he was a man who enjoyed a certain amount of conflict in his personal and professional life, and like his grandfather, was not averse to meddling with the truth to serve his own ends.

The main staircase at Faenol photographed before restoration. The design is typical of the early seventeenth century, however this particular variation is a local one, replicated in other local houses and probably produced by the same craftsman.

This panel shows the construction of the interior walls in the house. Wattle and daub was the plasterboard of its day.

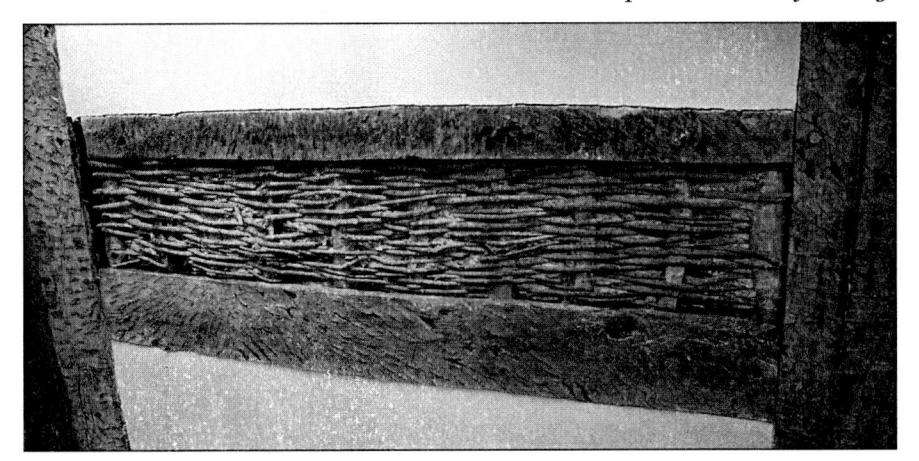

Documents recording Thomas as Sir Thomas appear from 1626 onwards (the year in which he served as High Sheriff of Caernarfonshire), so it seems clear that his father William died around that time. However, the will was not proved at the Consistory Court of Canterbury until 1630. This would seem a long time, but once again it appears that the Williams family were involved in some form of skulduggery where land was concerned. During the law suits over Robert Wynn's will, which contested land rents and who should and who had profited from them, Sir Thomas Williams stated to Chancery in 1627 that he was neither executor nor administrator of the estates of his father or stepmother, and furthermore that before his father's death William had made the estate over to Thomas and that there was no proper will.[18] Professor Carr, who wrote an article on the affairs of Robert Wynn warns us that we must be wary of taking these lawsuits with which the gentry diverted themselves at face value. They were as much about family rivalries, struggles for local power and even revenge as they were about land.[19] There is without doubt more than a whiff of deception about Sir Thomas Williams' role in the proceedings, for after more than thirty years of law suits had been concluded by a decree issued by the Court of Chancery in 1630, Sir William Williams' will was then proved in the same year. Not only was there therefore a properly witnessed will after all, but it also named Sir Thomas as the sole executor of that will. Twist of fate or twist of truth, we shall never know which.

Back in 1626, Sir Thomas may have considered it unfortunate that his arch enemy, Sir John Wynn and his great ally, Sir William Thomas, were joint deputy lieutenants of the shire, putting Sir John in a position to give him orders as High Sheriff of Caernarfonshire. It seems likely that John Wynn was behind the 'tumult and ryott' that surrounded Lady Dorothy Williams' alleged modified oath, and so it is ironic that Wynn passed on instructions from the Bishop of St Asaph to Williams to disarm all Papists in a number of areas around St Asaph.[20] Being High Sheriff of Caernarfonshire undoubtedly brought kudos but also brought this kind of additional work without financial recompense.

One could only stand for the position if money was not a problem and, even if he did not have the influence to be deputy lieutenant of the shire, the forty-year-old Sir Thomas had waited a long time to take on his father's mantle and Sir William had twice been high sheriff, in addition to being twice appointed a justice of the peace. Sir Thomas had the family reputation to uphold.

Perhaps his judgement was not as sound as his father's, or perhaps Thomas was plain unlucky, for later in the year he overstepped the mark when he meddled in the affairs of the Bishop of Bangor and found himself committed to the Fleet Prison in London. Historian A. H. Dodd tells us that Bishop Lewis Bayley was a thorn in the side of the local gentry and his enemies tried to get him impeached around this time. A dossier was compiled relating his alleged misdemeanours and it attacks Bayly as a 'slanderer of men of standing and a 'common striker' of both men and women.' Among those alleged to have suffered at the bishop's hands had been Sir William Williams and Thomas, as high sheriff, put out a warrant for the arrest of Bayley and his servant but was 'sent to the Lords on a charge of contempt' for his pains.[21]

Letters from other Caernarfonshire men, then living in London, flew back and forth to their families and associates back home all the time. From these we find that Sir Thomas petitioned the House of Lords for his freedom citing ill-health and matters of business in Caernarfonshire as reasons for his liberation from the Fleet. Sir Roger Mostyn, his old adversary, confirmed that 'Sir Thomas Williams is very sick.'[22] Eventually, word came from Owen Wynn in London, reporting to his father, Sir John, that the Bishop of Bangor put in a plea for Williams' discharge and he was released.[23] A letter from another Wynn ally (Sir William Thomas of Coed Helen in Caernarfon) further noted that Williams was 'admonished to acknowledge the Bishop's favour' in pressing for his release.[24] Unfortunately, Thomas Williams' feelings on the matter are unrecorded, although he did recover from the pleaded illness to live for a further ten years.

Trouble came naturally to the Williams family, but we must not think that it confined itself to the men. A few years earlier, in 1623,

Caernarfonshire society had had cause for gossip when Sir Thomas's cousin, Jane, secretly married the third son of Thomas Trafford, His Majesty's Receiver General for North Wales. Trouble ensued and the newly weds felt the wrath of Jane's father, Simon Williams of Wîg. Historian Norman Tucker noted that the Traffords were a Catholic family so it may have been that they were felt unsuitable in such politically and religiously volatile times.[25] On 23 September that year Owen Wynn at Caernarfon wrote gleefully to his father, Sir John Wynn, at Gwydir, that Simon Williams was irate at this clandestine union and had roundly insulted the Traffords at Beaumaris.[26] As Jane was Simon's sole heir it is safe to assume that his anger stemmed from his having other plans for her marital alliance since, although daughters had to be found a good dowry to attract the right husband, they could be very useful in cementing business connections with a good family, or even within one's own family. Girls were meant to do as they were told; Jane, however, appears to have followed her heart and risked her father's ire. One wonders who assisted her in being able to attend the secret ceremony; perhaps it was held near Trafford's home at Eglwyseg in Denbighshire, so that Jane's family did not get wind of it, and if so, how did she get there unhindered? There is certainly a hint of a romantic novel about the situation, although perhaps these things are more romantic in the telling than they are in the living. Thomas Trafford, her husband, clearly did well for a third son and later we see them both in dealings with their cousin Henry Williams (Sir Thomas Williams of Faenol's brother) over land in Dyffryn Conwy.[27] By 1631, the role of Receiver General had come down to Thomas Trafford through his family, an influential character in north Wales society, even if not much liked by his in-laws.

At Faenol, Sir Thomas and Lady Katherine spent time and money making their mark on their immediate environment. In the Old Hall garden today a gateway bears a date stone from the year 1633. This gateway was not however built as part of the wall, but created out of two stone external doorframes retained from a now demolished building and placed back to back. It is likely that these doorways were

The 1633 date stone above the garden gateway with the initials T W K (Thomas and Katherine Williams).

originally part of an eleven-roomed gatehouse that once stood in that area of the garden. Perhaps they formed entrances into the building from either side of the arched passage beneath the gatehouse.

Gatehouses were not then placed at the entrance to a long grand driveway, but rather opened directly into a courtyard, bounded by garden walls or other buildings, and the main residence. Often the family home was sited opposite the gatehouse so as to make maximum dramatic impact on arrival, framed like a painting by the gateway. These gatehouses were very fashionable in Thomas and Katherine's day, and while not needed as a defensive measure as in a medieval castle, were indispensable for announcing wealth and status to the caller as he rode up to the gate on his horse, arrived in a rumble of carriage wheels or made his way up to the house on foot (the route of the drive then being across the field from the main road at Capel-y-Graig). Some properties had modestly-sized gatehouses with a few rooms while others, like the one at Faenol, were much larger. Exactly which of the Williams generations built this gatehouse at Faenol is not known, but on the evidence of the date stone it would not be unreasonable to suggest that, if Thomas and Katherine did not build it themselves, they perhaps extended or embellished it. Faenol Old Hall was a sizeable building, but it was no mansion, and the additional rooms in the gatehouse proved useful for the accommodation of senior staff and the family chaplain who officiated when the Faenol Chapel was in use, and perhaps also led the family in prayers at mealtimes.

This gatehouse was demolished during the Victorian period or even possibly as late as the Edwardian era, when the old hall garden was redesigned by Lady Sybil Assheton Smith. Lady Sybil had a liking for the style of the old house and even had a fashionable Jacobean-style room created in the newer Faenol Hall. Perhaps the gatehouse was in an irreparable state because her fondness for this style can be seen in the design for the Dairy Cottage (which was no doubt influenced by the Arts and Crafts Movement) as well as the buildings in its immediate vicinity over which she had a great deal of design control, and which itself appears to boast a genuine seventeenth-century chimney which may have come from the gatehouse. The architectural inspirations of the Arts and Crafts Movement were by their very nature particularly sympathetic to the style of the Old Hall and the St Mary Chapel and it is quite likely that Lady Sybil retained the stone door frames from the gatehouse specifically for use in her garden scheme, adding her own loving message to them along with her initials.[28]

The other clue to Sir Thomas and Lady Katherine's building plans can be seen in the entrance lobby at the present-day Plas Dinorwic hotel, which stands upon a promontory above the dock at Felinheli at the far end of Faenol Park. Plas Dinorwic was built in the nineteenth century as a residence for the estate's quarry manager, but at sometime a date stone bearing Thomas and Katherine's initials and the date 1633 has been inserted into the porch wall. It is quite likely that this date stone came from the seventeenth-century seawater-powered mill from which the village of Felinheli takes its name (literally salt-water mill). This mill was owned by the Williams family and, although its origins are not certain, it may have been built or altered by Sir Thomas. Like the gatehouse, the mill no longer exists and was in disrepair by the 1700s. Comparisons with old maps suggest that Plas Dinorwic was built on the promontory above the mill site and that the mill site itself has disappeared under the dock extensions made by the owners of the Faenol estate in the late nineteenth century.[29] Perhaps the date stone found its way to Plas Dinorwic at this time.

The year 1634 may have been an expensive one for the Williams family. On 6 February, Thomas and Katherine's only daughter, twenty-three-year-old Magdalen, was married to Lewis Anwyl, a gentleman fifteen years her senior and recently widowed. Although they were never to have a child together, they raised Lewis' young daughter, Catherine, from his first marriage, as their own. After their marriage the couple seem to have lived at Faenol until the beginning of August, when, as Lewis records, 'I left Vaynol and together with my wife Magdalen came to live at Kemmes' [Cemaes]. At Christmas, Lewis recalls that he and his wife went to stay with 'the ladye Williams' (presumably Katherine) in Chester.[30] If this was Lady Katherine with whom they were staying, then it would suggest that the Williamses had taken some kind of accommodation in the city. With the roads in Caernarfonshire notoriously impassable in the winter, it is not surprising that those who could afford to do so took lodgings in the relative metropolis of Chester. During bad weather, even the gentry in rural areas could be virtual prisoners in their own homes. Magdalen's stay with her mother was longer than intended; illness kept her in Chester for several months until she was eventually well enough to manage the three-day carriage journey back to Cemaes at Whitsuntide. Carriages in those days were by no means as sophisticated in their suspension as they would become and coupled with the unmetalled roads, where pot holes jolted and jiggled passengers unrelentingly, and

The date stone from the tidal mill, the Felin Heli, from which the nearby village took its name.

perilous natural hazards such as the cliff road at Penmaenmawr had to be endured, it is no wonder that Magdalen put the journey off until both the weather and her health improved.

Two years later, Sir Thomas Williams, aged only fifty, succumbed to illness, dying in his bed at Faenol as the dawn broke on a Sunday morning, 26 June 1636. Lewis Anwyl recalled that his father-in-law was interred in the family tomb at Bangor Cathedral at night 'without either funeral sermon or other commemoracion'. Night-time burials were very fashionable at that time, a trend that had originally started with the aristocrats at the Royal Court who wished to avoid the high cost of the funerals expected of their class, and also to avoid the curious gaze of the men in the street at their time of mourning. Like so many other things, this had spread over time to become the way many wealthy families throughout England and Wales conducted funeral arrangements.

After her husband's death Katherine retired to the family's dower house, a property called Pryscol, near Llanrug, leaving her eldest son William to preside at Faenol. Dower houses were for many centuries the solution to a landed-family's problem of what to do with the lady of the house after her husband had died and the next generation were ready to take over the estate.[31] Katherine remained at Pryscol until her own death, aged about fifty-one, just three years later on the 14 November 1639. Lewis Anwyl is at pains to note the time of death as being 'between nine and ten of the clocke att night.' Like her husband, Lady Katherine was interred in the vault at the cathedral three days after her death, again at night and with no funeral service. Lewis Anwyl is very specific about there being no funeral service on either occasion, but perhaps there was a private service in the Faenol Chapel at a later date with the family chaplain.

Chapter 4
Sir William Williams, 3rd Baronet

Lewis Anwyl writes that at the time of Sir Thomas' death in 1636, Sir William was in France. He was not the only young gentleman from north Wales spending time across the Channel – other heirs to north Wales estates also made the trip. It is no great leap of the imagination to suppose that these young men had embroiled themselves in the machinations of the devastating European conflict known as the Thirty Years War – winning their spurs in battle, rather than learning the ways of estate management from their fathers. If this is the case then they may have found this experience of more use than they could have imagined during the Civil War which would later plague their time as owners of their various estates. Service in a foreign army would have been a somewhat different experience than if they had gone for the cultural sights of Europe and, whatever their reason for going, it would have no doubt broadened the educated minds of these provincial young men considerably and we can be sure that they brought back souvenirs of their time on the Continent. In a later document, we are referred to a watch that Sir William 'kept and used himself'[32] and, bearing in mind that watch making was still a young art/science in this era and that Geneva was at the forefront of this movement in the 1620s and 30s, it may be that the watch was one such souvenir and it is not hard to imagine him feigning a casual stance back home as he consulted this item in company, demonstrating his keeping up with the latest in technology.

In 1636, Sir William came home to Faenol as a single man in his twenties; a wealthy and influential man who took over the role of High Sheriff of Caernarfonshire, as well as ownership of the Faenol estate. However, bachelors do not create legitimate heirs and in April 1640, he made a very good marital liaison with a woman named Margaret Jones, the eldest daughter and co-heiress of a powerful Penllŷn family, Jones of Castellmarch. Her father, Griffith Jones, was an influential man in the area who would later hold the important position of *Custos Rotulorum*[33] for the county of Caernarfonshire, and her paternal grandfather, Sir William Jones, was Chief Justice of the King's Bench in Ireland and later in England, under King Charles I.[34] Her maternal grandfather, William Gruffith, was a gentleman from Caernarfon who resided at Plas Mawr, one of the walled town's largest houses.[35] William Gruffith inherited the use of the private chapel at Llanbeblig Church in Caernarfon, which had been built on to the main church by his grandfather. Through Margaret Jones' marriage to Sir William Williams of Faenol, the chapel came into the hands of the Faenol estate, and is still known as the Faenol Chapel, over 400 years later. Here you can see the altar tomb of William Gruffith and his wife, their likenesses carved in stone for eternity.

When Margaret Jones and Sir William Williams of Faenol were married, her father and two grandfathers came together to decide how all their land should be divided up for the future. Margaret and her sister Jane were the sole rightful heirs to this land, there being no male

Castellmarch, near Abersoch, the home of the powerful Jones family.

Llanbeblig Church, Caernarfon. [Ryan Jones]

heirs for the combined lands of these three powerful men. This resulting document details thousands of acres of land that Margaret brought to her marriage with William, and as Wales had been under English land law for a century, this meant that her land became the property of William, and therefore part of the Faenol estate. The influence of the Faenol estate now stretched from Dyffryn Conwy in the north to Penllŷn in the south.

We know little of what was happening at Faenol Hall at this time, apart from the daily life of a gentleman's house. Visitors of rank were entertained in the 'dyneing roome' so expensively furnished by William's grandfather less than twenty years before. These visitors would often stay over, particularly if the weather and the roads were bad. There would be rooms furnished to a standard that such visitors would expect, chambers where they could sleep, sit at a table to eat privately or conduct some business, as well as the Williams family chambers and staff quarters in the attics and in the gatehouse.

The kitchens in the basement would be kept busy feeding family and guests, as well as staff, visiting staff accompanying the guests and probably a variety of calling tradesmen. At certain times of the year, when rents were due, or the harvest secured, tenants could expect to be treated to a feast. Unlike her nineteenth-century counterpart, the lady of the seventeenth-century gentry house would have had a great deal of input into and overseeing of what went on in the kitchens and in the preparation of staples such as cheese, butter and beer. Lady Margaret would have been involved in the preparation of medicines and household items such as cleaning products and ink for writing. Recipes for items such as these were often handed down from mother to daughter in preparation for marriage.[36]

One snapshot into the social life of the Williamses of Faenol Old Hall comes from a letter written at Christmas 1642 by Archbishop John Williams from his home at Penrhyn near Llandegai, Bangor. He informs the recipient that he was 'engaged in so many visits and feasts at Tom Bulkeley's [at Baron Hill, Beaumaris] and Sir William Williams' [Faenol] that it [would] be twelve days at least before [he could] leave these parts.'[37] A later diarist would lament that Faenol Old Hall had been a place of conviviality and mirth in its heyday.[38] Business and

Christmas feasts in gentry houses were lavish affairs with several courses and tables groaning with food. The decorated pigs head would have taken centre stage, surrounded by gleaming gold-leafed fruit and sweetmeats and other complicated dishes designed to demonstrate the technical competence of the cook and budget allocated to the kitchen, as well as in celebration of the holy day. [Tony Jones]

pleasure mixed easily with family life, and times were good for William and his estate.

But all this feasting should not keep us from the more sinister events going on outside the door, even in these rural parts of Wales. The conflict between King and Parliament held everyone's attention and news sheets (the forerunners of newspapers) were passed from town to town to be avidly read and discussed. By 1642, civil war had broken out and would reach into every corner of England and Wales.

The Civil War
During the Civil War Sir William Williams (3rd Baronet) did his best to protect his interests and those of the county. He began the war like so many others in the area as a Royalist and in 1642 King Charles I included him in Caernarfonshire's Commission of Array; a working party to organize troops and military needs in the area. As there was no standing army at this period; soldiers were raised as the need arose and Sir William wrote many letters during this period making arrangements and sorting out problems.

However, with all the initial battles of the war taking place in England, the King demanded that troops and ordnance be sent from north Wales to where they were needed. King Charles I wrote to the Commissioners of the Array and Sir William Williams repeatedly during 1642 requesting men, money and arms.[39] The Caernarfonshire Gentry, in particular Sir William and some of his fellow Commissioners, were very concerned about this state of affairs which left north Wales with little defence if Parliamentarian troops should break through the English/Welsh border. Perhaps more worrying still, the situation left them completely vulnerable should the enemy attack from the sea as there were many beaches along this coastline where troops could be landed from ships and both Royalist and Parliamentarian ships patrolled these waters throughout the war. The Commissioners of Array were very reluctant to accede to the King's demands and before long, he wrote to them to complain that some people in their area were more interested in looking after private concerns than the national interest.[40] In fact, even while in service of the king, some of the Commissioners were later to show their true colours as staunch Parliamentarian supporters, but Sir William cannot have been alone in his desire to protect his assets and concerns. Many estate owners throughout England and Wales trod a careful path at this time with the safe and continued future of their estate a primary concern if it was to remain in the hands of their family for generations to come.

In 1644 the King appointed Sir William and the Sheriff, Robert Jones, to raise horse and foot for the trained band. In the following January, the local colonels were ordered by the Commissioners of Array to 'issues warrants to their several captains to have their companies ready to march with a thousand men to Conwy, 'and from thence to the confines of Denbighshire, there to attend the motions of the rebels'.[41] That spring three or four thousand Royalist soldiers saw action on the Flintshire/Cheshire border where the Parliamentarian Colonels Brereton and Myddleton were laying siege to a series of important castles and walled towns such as Chester, and the castles at Beeston and Hawarden. The news pamphlets of the time show Sir William, ranked as Colonel Williams, involved in fighting himself at this time, and was no doubt there, mounted on horseback when the Royalist forces managed to temporarily drive the Parliamentarians out of Flintshire and Denbighshire. However, in April 1646, the Parliamentarians were back and this time reached as far into Caernarvonshire as Penrhyn Hall[42] where Sir William's 'cozen' the Royalist Archbishop Williams was living. The stories variously have it that the Archbishop found the Parliamentarian general, Mytton, far more courteous than the brusque Royalist Lord Byron or perhaps the latter's 'predatory troopers' made themselves unwelcome at Penrhyn. Norman Tucker relates how once 'Lord Byron established himself in Caernarfon in the spring of 1646 the county felt the rough grasp of his avaricious hand ... [despatching] parties of war-hardened veterans to collect money for his depleted war chest.'[43] Something certainly

Facing: Sir William Williams' 'cozen', the Royalist Archbishop John Williams. A 1642 satirical engraving by Wenceslas Hollar.

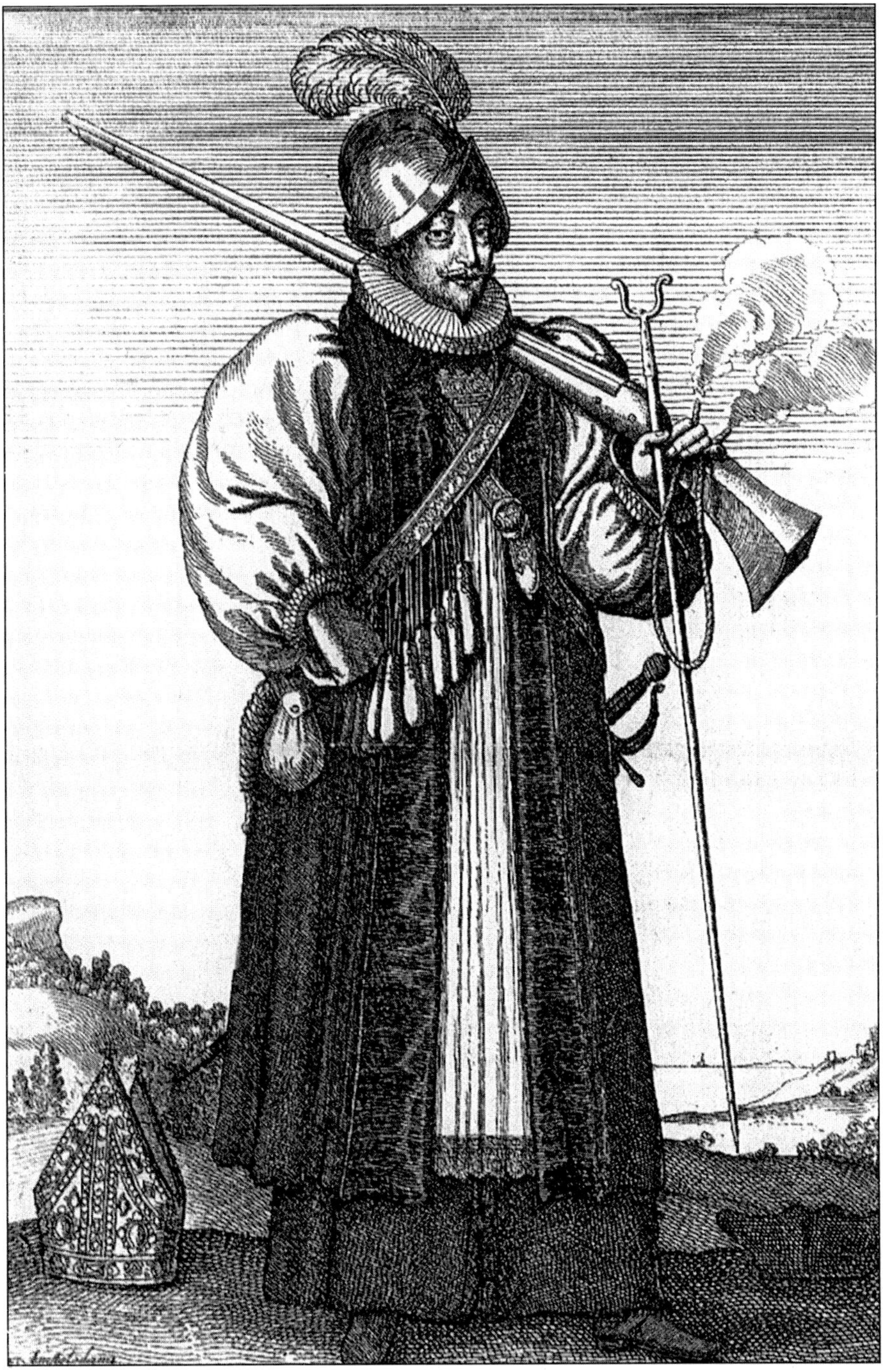

persuaded that previously staunch follower of the King, Archbishop John, to change sides to favour the Parliamentarian party.

The very next month, Sir William was amongst those who followed suit. We know he was on good terms with the Archbishop who had spent a genial Christmas feasting at Faenol in 1642. Possibly, the Archbishop had persuaded his cousin to join the opposing side, or perhaps Sir William had needed no persuading as he had not been best pleased with the King's policy regarding Caernarvonshire. In addition, since 1640 Sir William had been the son-in-law of his good friend and staunch Parliamentarian, Griffith Jones. William and Griffith had been on the King's Commission of Array together back in 1642 and it may be that his father-in-law's influence was another contributory factor in his apparent change of heart. Parliamentary propaganda claimed that Sir William 'was very forward to afford the General [Mytton] all accommodations fortifying also his house against the Lord Byron.'[44] Whether this means that Faenol was fortified in the sense of a garrison or whether simply the gates were barred, pistols, pikes and pitchforks at the ready to repel Royalist troops, we do not know. It is unlikely that there was any sort of major skirmish on Faenol grounds in the vicinity of the house; the Civil War prompted a great outpouring of printed material in terms of news sheets and propaganda leaflets and any serious confrontation would doubtless have made it to the pages of these.

In the same month, May 1646, the Parliamentarians laid siege to Caernarfon Castle and the propaganda machine notes Sir William amongst the gentry turned besiegers. Later, in 1647, when Caernarvonshire was under Parliamentary control, these actions would mean that Sir William, and his fellow 'turncoats' would be excused their earlier Royalist sympathies. In April of that year he was elected on to the newly-formed Parliamentarian Assessment Committee for Caernarvonshire, whose job it was to assess the taxes and fines payable to the Parliament by the county. Later still, 'turning coat' would mean that Sir William's estate suffered no fines or sequestration[45] under the Commonwealth government, despite events still to come.

The grass is rarely greener on the other side and there was increasing discontent in the county. The continued presence of troops and horse was a terrible drain on the finances of a county trying to settle back down into some form of economic normality. Archbishop John Williams succeeded in persuading General Mytton to reduce the garrisons in the county and the unneeded Roundhead soldiers were gradually paid off and sent home. Inevitably, the Parliamentarians were starting to lose their shine, particularly the governor of Conwy, Colonel John Carter, whom Dodd describes as being 'blatantly on the make and soon became the most unpopular man in North Wales.'[46]

Amongst the gentry of the shire some of the principal die-hard Parliamentarians were now dead, whilst under Sir John Owen of Clennennau, the Royalist cause and insurrections against the occupying power, whilst ultimately to be disappointed, were rekindled. By early 1648 there were only a few of the Caernarvonshire gentry left who inwardly supported the Parliament. And what of Faenol? Although Sir William had been appointed to a position within the Parliamentarian local government in 1647, he was one of those whom Carter condemned as privately supporting the insurrections against Parliament. Later in 1648, his inclinations of the moment were very much on display when he fought, once again, on the side of the Royalists at the battle on the seashore at Y Dalar Hir, near Llandegai.

Despite this return to the Royalist side, Sir William appears to have still been considered a trustworthy candidate for reappointment to the High Sheriff of Caernarfonshire under the rule of Oliver Cromwell and the Commonwealth; a role he shouldered once more in 1654.

However, Sir William's life, both as a public servant and a private estate owner, came to a close on 1st November 1658. His had been an eventful life, featuring as it did both European travel and warfare, but no doubt as he looked down from the afterlife, he would have regretted that he missed the opportunity to see a monarch restored to the throne of Britain by only two years, and the drama surrounding his father-in-law's kidnap by pirates in the pay of Royalists by one year.[47] Sir William must only have been in his late forties when he died, which by our standards is no age at all, but was not an uncommon age for even a gentleman to die in the seventeenth century. His will gives no hint of what he died from, only the standard line that he was 'weake in body but of good and perfecte memorie'. The format of William's will is interesting in that it was made during the period when there was no monarch on the throne and the government of the Anglican Church by bishops and by deans and chapters had been banished. This meant that there was no elaborate praising of any British figurehead at the start of the document, only a commendation of his soul to Almighty God and a belief that his sins would be pardoned by doing so. He asks for his body to be laid in his own vault in the late Cathedral Church of Bangor – 'late' in the sense that there was no longer a diocese in which for it to be the principal church or cathedral.

We know from William and Margaret's marriage settlement that the Faenol estate had increased significantly in size during the 1640s, with a particular concentration now around Caernarfon. How much buying and selling of land between the gentry of Caernarfonshire went on during the period of the Civil War is not easy to say; normal life and the business of agriculture and trade had been much disrupted and the inability of farmers and drovers to move their livestock to the markets of England where they made their money had been well nigh impossible. Much hardship was felt at the lower end of the social scale and it must have been difficult for them to pay their rents. Once hostilities had ceased however, those estate owners who had come through the war with their estates more or less intact were able to benefit from the renewed activity in the livestock trade and normal life was resumed, albeit under the sober strictures of the Cromwell and the Puritan regime.

Death was never very far away in the seventeenth century and only seven years into their marriage (1647), Sir William had lost his wife Margaret Jones, leaving only one surviving small child, their son and heir Griffith. Soon, as was the way, William had married again, to another Margaret, this time the daughter of the Melai branch of the notorious Wynn family. One heir is never really enough to guarantee the continuation of the family line and doubtless William and his new wife hoped for children. It was not to be, and he speaks of his regret about this through the formal language of his will: '... it hath not pleased God to bestowe me with any issue [children] by my now wife'.

With the entire future of the Faenol estate resting on the shoulders of one small boy, Sir William must have hoped for at least one more son from his second wife. Nevertheless, he took comfort from '... her greate love and affection towards mee and alsoe her paynes in ordering my house and familie'.

He refers to Margaret as his loving wife, and those of his family and friends whom he appointed as executors he describes as 'deare' and 'loveing'. This picture he paints of a happy and harmonious group of people is somewhat cautioned by a sentence earlier on in the document where he writes: '... for and touching whatt temporall state[48] the Lord hath been pleased to bestowe upon mee and for the settlings thereof whereby noe strife or confrontation may happen amongst my surviving friends about the same ...'[49] Did he foresee trouble ahead and was he hoping to avoid it by reminding people of their love for him (if not for each other) and of his love for them?

As usual, we read in Sir William's will about the 'left-overs'; his bequests that fall outside the main body of the Faenol estate entailed for the next generation. To his wife Margaret it is interesting to see that amongst other items he leaves, 'my messuages, lands and tenements, houses, shoppes, barnes, stables, gardens, orchards [and] banksides [situated] in the parish of Llanbeblike and within the towne and liberties of Carnarvon.'

These were properties that he had given her during his lifetime and he reiterates that she was to keep them as part of her dower. The beauty of the words is that that they create a picture of Caernarfon and its environs for us; a place where people live, work and shop, farm and grow fruit. The banksides probably represent rights on the river Seiont, perhaps as it wends its way through the countryside, or even as it widens out into the port of Caernarfon itself. They were a part of what was listed as a portion of the dowry that had come with Margaret, his first wife, from her maternal grandfather William Gruffith, and although they later became part of his second wife's dower, Sir William knew that they would come back to the use of the Faenol estate itself on her death. Other glimpses into the daily life of the household also come from this document too – the salary of twenty pounds per annum, in addition to a gift of forty pounds, to be given to his son Griffith's tutor, John, and varying sums to a whole host of servants, including Simon Codcroft, his cook, and a lady called Gwen, so obviously a part of their lives that she needed no identification by surname. Attached to a later agreement was a 'particular of the legacies and of the knowne debts of Sir William Williams, deceased ...' From this, we can glean some further insights into the people who made up the Faenol household. The senior household staff were male, as was usual then and, like Simon the cook, the steward John Evans was left five pounds by his former employer. Even the undercook, John Thomas, was left one pound. These sums were no trifling amounts in 1658 and it suggests that Sir William was a man who appreciated his staff and was by no means ungenerous.

Of all the people left behind, the most important now becomes Sir William's only child, named after his maternal grandfather, Griffith. Not yet even seventeen, Griffith had lost both his natural parents, although Margaret, his stepmother, still lived. This however, seems to have been of little comfort to the young man and almost as soon as his father died, Sir Griffith and his step-mother began to argue over the terms of Sir William's will. Fortunately, his grandfather, Griffith Jones (of Castellmarch), was also still around to act as mediator and to ensure that 'Dame Margarett, her executors or administrators shall be noe further molested, impeached or trubled by the said Sir Griffith Williams, his heirs or administrators'. This extract from the agreement which would later be drawn up between them, implies that Sir Griffith had been trying to prevent her from having access to her dower.

Dame (or Lady) Margaret was a daughter of landowner John Wynn of Melai, previously identified as another branch of the powerful Wynn family of Gwydir. The Williamses of Faenol and Cochwillan and the Wynns of Gwydir had long been great antagonists, vying with each other for power and influence. In 1593, for example, Conwy Parish Church had been the venue for one such altercation between William Williams of Cochwillan and Sir John Wyn of Gwydir. A disagreement over subsidy levies descended into actual blows being exchanged in the church before the whole situation had been put before the Court of Star Chamber in Westminster, which found in favour of Williams. Nevertheless, this did not prevent them from forming these marital alliances. Unfortunately, the marital alliances did not prevent further strife and in fact Dame Margaret had written to Richard Wynn, High Sheriff of Caernarfonshire, just a few months before Sir William's death, with regard to the termination of unfriendly relations between her relative Wynn and her husband.[50] Now there was a strife brewing between herself and her confident young stepson that Sir William had hoped to avoid.

Chapter 5
Sir Griffith Williams, 4th Baronet

On 13 January 1659, Sir Griffith Williams, Griffith Jones and Dame Margaret Williams put their seals to a document agreeing the terms by which the will of Sir William Williams would be interpreted.[51] Judging by the number of Wynns who bore witness to this document, Dame Margaret had the backing of her family for her side and, although the young Griffith seems to have been nobody's fool, it was perhaps as well that he had his family reputation, not to mention that of his grandfather supporting his part. This had been no minor disagreement and thirteen people signed the document as witnesses. Knowing the Williams and Wynn predilection for arguments, this would have been a well thrashed-out set of agreements and compromises.

Whether Sir William knew of the antipathy between his second wife and his son we cannot know. He did not make provision however as to where she would live after his death. Perhaps such things were understood, after all the Faenol estate habitually used Pryscol at Llanrug as a dower house, where Sir William's own mother, Dame Katherine, had lived out her years. Given that Dame Margaret would live until the end of the century there may not have been many years between her and her stepson and perhaps she felt herself too young to be pensioned off to the dower house at Pryscol. As his father's heir, perhaps young Sir Griffith felt he should have become head of the household at Faenol on William's death, but the agreement tells us that Griffith Williams was under seventeen-years-of-age at the time and as an unmarried minor may not have been considered suitable as the head of the household by his elders, no matter what the young man himself thought. The agreement unequivocally states that 'Dame Margarett shall have such use and benefitt of the capitall messuage in Vaynol for the habitation and being of herselfe, her attendants and servants.' Translated into plain speak this means that Margaret was to live in the Old Hall, with her own staff, as head of household. Where Sir Griffith was to live until his coming of age is not specified, but perhaps, given the ill-feeling between him and his step-mother, he lived with one of his guardians, possibly his grandfather.

If he did indeed live with his grandfather, then he would have witnessed, at first hand, the kidnap of this Parliamentarian gentleman from his home at Castellmarch near Abersoch, by Captain John Bartlett who was in the pay of the Royalists. Jones was whisked away to Wexford in Ireland, leaving his wife to send panic-stricken messages to her Williams in-laws. With William Williams of Faenol being dead and Griffith a mere boy, the call was answered by William's brother Thomas of Plas Dinas, Bontnewydd and by Faenol's near neighbour Richard Griffith of Plas Llanfair. Richard and Thomas sped on horseback the thirty-mile journey to Castellmarch to find the pirates still ransacking the house and Griffith Jones long departed on the ship to Ireland. Only the tearful pleadings of the lady of the house spared the lives of the marauders whom the vengeful men would have put to the sword. Thus thwarted, the gentlemen put their energies into ensuring the safe return of the elderly Griffith. It took a great deal of negotiation with the Royalists holding him, and eventually only an agreement for a swap of high status prisoners saw Griffith's release. It is generally considered that it was the release of the prominent local Royalist, Sir John Owen, that secured his freedom. Although Griffith Jones continued to serve on county committees under Cromwell, he came to feel that life without the King was not necessarily greener and eventually he found himself in favour of the return of the monarchy. Despite this, after the Restoration he did spend a short time in Caernarfon gaol, suspected of dubious political allegiances. Eventually however, his star must have risen again and he became High Sheriff of Caernarfonshire in 1663.

Meanwhile, six years passed, a long time in Sir Griffith Williams' life, a period of Faenol history which is closed to us. During this time, a bride had been sought and found, and on 25 July 1665, Sir Griffith, now a young man in his early twenties, married Penelope Bulkeley from the powerful Baron Hill family. A marriage settlement was agreed between Griffith and Penelope's brother, Robert Lord Bulkeley, and other relatives including Sir Roger Mostyn of Mostyn, another very influential landowner in north Wales. This settlement shows the great extent of the Faenol estate by this time, a massive twenty-three thousand acres. This was by no means all unusable mountainous wastes, but included 6,000 acres of meadow, 6,000 acres of pasture and 500 acres of wood; all integral parts of the system of farming. In addition to this, Sir Griffith also owned seven mills, two pigeon houses (presumably to supply meat for his own table), three piscaries and three weirs (for the catching or trapping of fish). The newly-weds would by no means struggle for a steady income from the rents of these possessions.

On their marriage, if not before, Sir Griffith would have taken his place at Faenol Old Hall and it is known that Dame Margaret did indeed move to the dower house at Pryscol at some point before her death in 1698. Given all that had gone on previously, the likelihood of her living with her stepson and daughter-in-law seems fairly remote. Although Griffith did not follow in his father's footsteps as High Sheriff, he was undoubtedly one of the wealthiest gentlemen in the county. As the standing army had been disbanded in these times of uneasy peace, King Charles II was very keen that all county militias be kept in readiness, should he need to defend his position. Gentlemen like Sir Griffith were obliged to provide the militia with a certain number of armed men and horses depending on their wealth. He was one of only five property owners considered wealthy enough to supply two horsemen to the county militia,[52] instead of one, being the more usual requirement.

Each new generation at Faenol undertook at least one building project that survives today. That Sir Griffith and Dame Penelope had capital to invest in building projects is demonstrated by the building of the extension to the Great Barn at Faenol, built fifty years before by

Sir Griffith's great-grandparents William and Dorothy. The sandstone datestone has all but worn away (a poor choice of stone for a permanent marker of their project) but it is still possible to make out the 'GW' and the 'P'. That it must have once marked a date in the 1660s is guaranteed by Griffith's untimely death in 1669. Given that he was less than seventeen years old in 1658, Sir Griffith must have been under thirty at his death and the extension to the barn newly finished. Little time enough for the young man to achieve much more than a building project and two sons. What plans he had for the estate we shall never know, but over a decade would come to pass before a Williams was back in charge of Faenol's future.

There is no record of a will for this young man who had lived through such eventful times; being born during the Civil War, hearing of the King restored to the throne of Britain and feuding with his stepmother and her family. However, a probate inventory (see Appendix 1) was taken on 8 July 1669, shortly after his death, which recorded all the moveable goods owned by the young baronet. This is a tremendous opportunity for us to peek into the Old Hall over 330 years ago but tells us nothing about why or how Sir Griffith died. A gentleman of such note would have had a will proved at the Prebendary Court of Canterbury, as did the other Williamses of Faenol. An official record of that will would have been kept at the Court, and indeed copies

Bodysgallen Hall, the home of Colonel Hugh Wynn.

Colonel Hugh Wynn

of his predecessors' wills may be found there. However, no record of Sir Griffith's will has so far been found and this suggests that he died suddenly with no time to record his final wishes – an accident, an infection or an illness that progressed swiftly and lethally? We shall probably never know. But it is an unfortunate truth that death wore a familiar face in the seventeenth century, and not long after her bereavement, his wife Penelope also suffered the loss of one of their young children, their eldest boy, Sir Thomas Williams, Fifth Baronet of Faenol.

After Sir Griffith's death, Penelope remarried, this time to Colonel Hugh Wynn of the Bodysgallen estate near Conwy. This was undoubtedly a good marriage within the expectations of the society in which they lived; in addition to being a landed gentleman, Colonel Wynn was a veteran officer of the Civil War. As to his desirability as a suitor, we can only guess; Wynn was a man of Penelope's parent's generation and, judging from his portrait, was no dashing, handsome officer of a girl's dreams!

As far as the Faenol estate was concerned, it temporarily became conjoined with Colonel Hugh's lands. Sir Griffith had been an only child and with the loss of his elder child Thomas this left the infant William as Griffith's heir and the sixth incumbent of the baronetcy. William's mother and step-father became not only William's guardians but also the possessors of Faenol until he should come of age to inherit. How much say Penelope had in how the estate should be managed is anyone's guess, but a document of September 1671 shows that parts of it, including the Old Hall, were leased to a man called Ellis Yonge of Bryn Iorkin in Flintshire.[53] The lease was to be held by Ellis Yonge until the deaths of Penelope and Hugh. Upon their deaths, the lease would have to be renegotiated between Yonge and whoever was Sir William's guardian, or even Sir William himself if he was of age, and of a mind to continue to lease his estate out, which seemed unlikely.

The death of one of the signatories to that lease came swifter than they could have imagined. Only four years after Sir Griffith's death, Penelope was also dead, leaving Sir William orphaned aged no more than eight-years-old. Even his long-lived great-grandfather Griffith Jones of Castellmarch had died two years previously in 1671. After such an inauspicious start in life, what could the future hold for the boy?

Chapter 6
Sir William Williams, 6th Baronet

Penelope left her remaining son in the care of his stepfather, Colonel Wynn, seeking the Colonel's permission to write a will, which is in essence her wishes for William:

[I] do hereby constitue and appoynt my husband my executor and doe grant and devise to him the [care?] and tuition of my Sonne and Heire Sir William Williams Baronett together with the mannagement of his estate during the minority of my said Sonne, trusting to my said Husband that he will carefully educate my said Sonne.

As we have seen, from its beginnings with Thomas Wyn ap Willim in the sixteenth-century, hard-headed business and financial dealings and canny marriages had grown the Faenol estate into a significant player in Caernarfonshire society. With this rise in influence and status, the property we know as Faenol Old Hall – that which Thomas Wyn ap Willim had referred to as 'my house at Vaynoll' – also grew, in both size and symbolic importance. The adjoining home farm was one of the largest and best equipped in the county and the Great Barn dominated the immediate landscape.[54] It was not uncommon for generations to be so short of heirs, but for Sir Griffith's father to have only one surviving child between two wives, and the deaths of Sir Griffith and his wife Penelope in their twenties, leaving only one surviving child of their own, is unfortunate by any estate's book. Who knows what might have been achieved had there been a more consistent line of descent.

Facing: The sea chart of the Menai Strait commissioned by Sir William Williams in 1696.

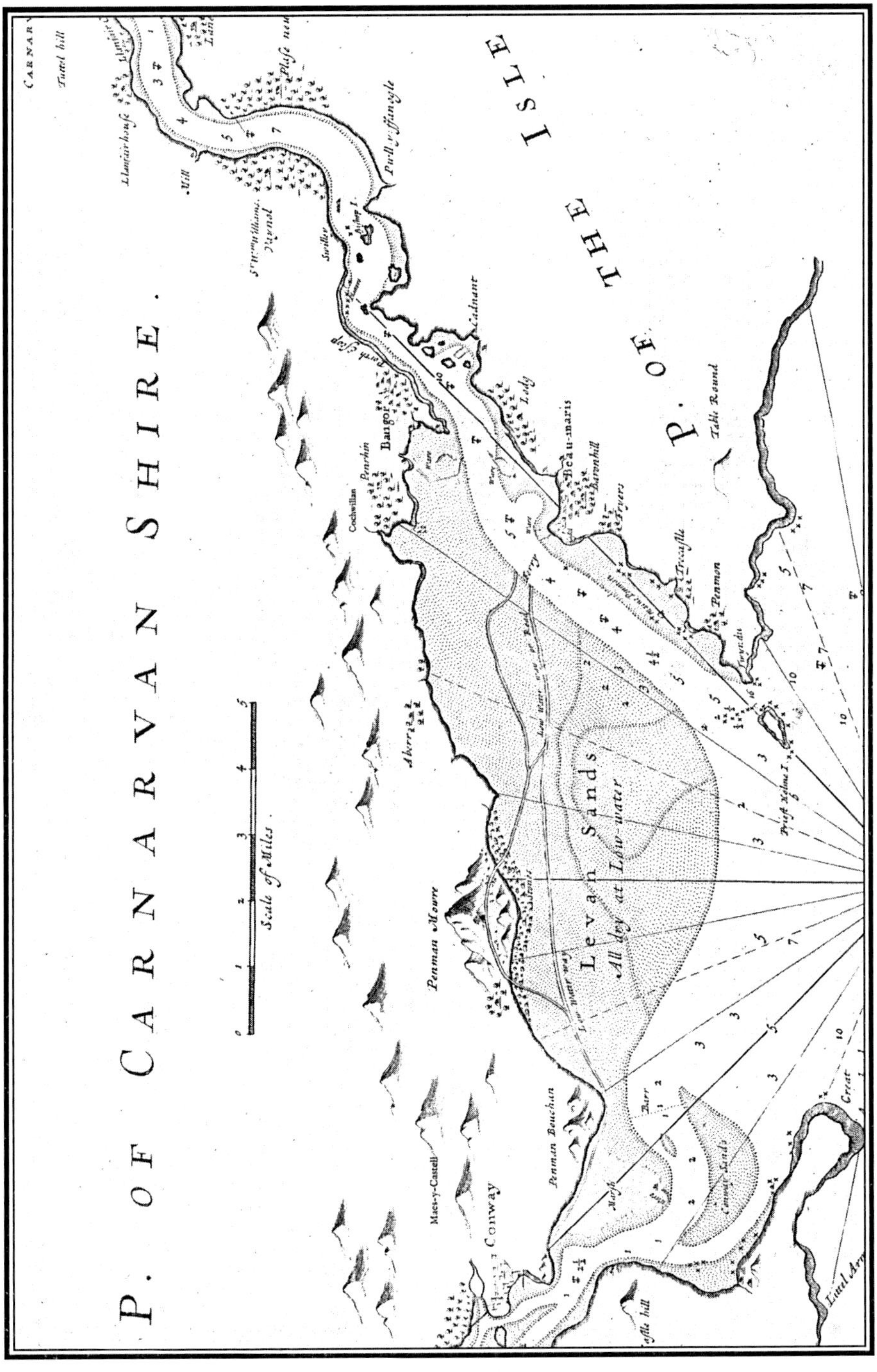
P. OF CARNARVAN SHIRE.
THE ISLE
P. OF
Scale of Miles
Levan Sands
All dry at Low-water
Bangor
Beau-maris
Conway
Penman Mawre
Penman Bouchan
Maes-y-Castell
Cochwillan
Penrhin
Priest Holme I.
Penmon
Table Round
Cadnant
Great

Whether due to the nature of ambition, policy or by circumstance, political ambition at the Faenol estate had been confined so far to local politics. So, when in 1689, Sir William Williams succeeded in gaining the county seat in Parliament it could be said that the business acumen and the political and marital liaisons of the five previous generations of the owners of the estate had finally come to political fruition.[55]

Although his mother's will put him under the protection of her husband Hugh Wynn, it seems that her own family, the Bulkeleys of Baron Hill took a great interest in the future of their young grandson. Indeed, Dodd tells us that in 1675 Lord Bulkeley was staying at Faenol prior to travelling triumphantly with his retinue to Caernarfon where he confidently expected to be returned as MP for the county. The Parliamentary historian Henning reports that 'under the ruling of his kinsman Heneage Finch [William] became the ward of his uncle',[56] Robert, second Viscount Bulkeley. What date this was is not clear, but by his late teens (around 1685) he was married to his cousin, Lord Bulkeley's daughter Ellen. There can be no firmer way of tying a young kinsman to your branch of the family line than by marrying him to your

The dedication from Sir William WIlliams' sea chart, displaying his heraldic arms.

daughter. While no marriage agreement appears to have survived, some of the Bulkeley estate must have been promised to William in dowry.

He could have been no more than twenty-three, when, under the guiding influence of Lord Bulkeley, Sir William Williams began his political career as a Justice of the Peace and Deputy Lieutenant of Caernarfonshire in 1688, cutting his judicial teeth in the courts of the Quarter Sessions. This was followed by his return as the Member of Parliament for Caernarfonshire in the following year. At the time he was in Parliament he was not the only Sir William Williams amongst the Members of the House. However, his namesake (brother-in-law to Arthur Owen, of whom we shall hear more later) seems to have had a much livelier interest in Parliamentary proceedings. Indeed most of the recorded contributions to debates in the Chamber are attributed to this other man. It should come as no surprise therefore that our Sir William's interests were not purely confined to politics although how much interest he showed in the affairs of his estate at Faenol is unknown.

Something that did interest Sir William greatly was naval affairs, something perhaps encouraged by Lord Bulkeley who was vice-admiral for Wales. When Lord Bulkeley died in October 1688, Sir William was appointed vice-admiral of Wales in his stead. His fascination with all things naval was such that in 1696, he commissioned a sea chart of the Menai Strait, ensuring that it featured not only the water ways, ferries and safe beach passages for those on foot, but also Faenol and some of the other major properties that bordered this stretch of water between Caernarfonshire and Anglesey.[57]

Someone, however, had greater ambitions for Sir William than a purely naval career and the young Tory baronet was returned again in 1690 and 1695 to the seat for Caernarfonshire. Being an MP was something only someone as wealthy as a substantial landowner could undertake and, although no records appear to exist regarding estate business for this period, we must believe that Sir William's political life was supported by the income from the estate at home in Caernarfonshire and Anglesey, estimated by Henning and Cruickshanks *et al* to be worth between £2,500 and £3,000.[58] While fortune had not smiled upon his father or elder brother, it had at least allowed the estate to increase in size to the point where it was significant enough to bear the substantial costs of political life. In terms of Caernarfonshire landed estates, Sir William was a considerable landowner, landlord and political influence by the end of the seventeenth-century. If fate had not stepped in once more and deprived the last baronet and his wife Lady Ellen of any heirs before his own premature death, there may have been structural changes to Faenol Old Hall to reflect the resurrection of the political prestige of the estate.

As will be seen, however, the life of a young gentleman and Member of Parliament was not directly commensurate with a life as a sober and upstanding citizen. Anecdotes of drinking, gambling and duelling were rife amongst his contemporaries and Sir William was no exception. His relationship with the Bulkeleys was obviously not at its best when in February 1692 he seconded his friend Sir Bourchier Wrey in a duel in Hyde Park with Thomas Bulkeley.[59] That Thomas only managed to slightly wound William may have been caused by the difficulties of accurately firing a flint-lock pistol. He may have been a poor shot or perhaps short-sighted, or might there have been more to it than that?

On his death in 1696, Sir William Williams can have been no more than thirty-years-old. A short life and perhaps not terribly productive, but we should not write him off completely; whatever his vices there is no suggestion that they were any worse than any of his contemporaries, and although he was to make the decision to end the line of Welsh ownership of the Faenol estate for a period that would turn out to be three hundred years, he may not have been as biddable as some of his friends may have liked. He left the estate to his friends the Wrey family of Tawstock in Devon, but his will states clearly that upon the death of all three Wreys, it was 'then unto and to the Use of our Sovereign Lord King William [III]' In anticipation of gaining control of the estate, King William issued a Letters Patent in 1669 in which he wrote:

Now know ye that We ... Have given and granted and by these present for ourselves our Heirs and Successors Do give and grant [the Faenol estate] unto our beloved and faithful Subject John Gore Esquire.*

In a deed dated 21 March 1699,[60] John Gore was elected to hold the estate in trust for one John Smith** and his heirs.[59] Later narratives declare that the estate was gifted by Queen Anne to 'Speaker Smith', however, this tale originates[61] with an unreliable source given to romantic notions, perhaps based on family hearsay. The existence of the letters patent and the deed poll proves undeniably that the fate of the Faenol estate was firmly and legally established before Queen Anne came to the throne. Yet, however nicely signed and sealed this may have been, it gives no indication of the *contretemps* that had been going on at Faenol since Sir William's death.

---

* It is not clear who this John Gore was or why he was chosen to hold the estate in trust for John Smith. One of the academics involved in the History of Parliament project hypotheses that he was the son of Sir John Gore (who died in 1697) who emigrated to Ireland and was Member of Parliament for Ennis in 1692–3. He later sat in the first short parliament of King William III and is described in Johnston Liik's *History of the Irish Parliament, 1692–1800* as a shadowy figure about whom there is little information.

** By the time William III gave the reversion of the Faenol estate to John Smith (known as the 'richest commoner in England') this gentleman had progressed from Member of Parliament to the post of Lord of the Treasury and then Chancellor of the Exchequer, a man whose star was very definitely on the rise. Five years later, he became a controversial appointment as Speaker of the House of Commons and was the first Speaker of the post-Act of Union Parliament of 1707. Prosperous landowners, the Smiths had a family seat at Tedworth in Hampshire and John Smith dismissed his newly acquired Welsh estate as a 'tract of bogs and rocks'. It was not until his great grandson, Thomas Assheton Smith, inherited the estate that Faenol began to show potential as a financial investment.

Chapter 7
Ungentlemanly Behaviour

After Sir William's death the unbroken line of Williams men as owners of the Faenol estate was irrevocably broken. This was by no means the end of the story, but it did bring a closure to a particular phase in the estate's history. When Dame Ellen heard of her husband's death in London in 1696 she can have had no immediate sense of the troubles that were to follow.

During 1697, a number of petitions were put before the House of Commons followed by a complete overview with witness statements, before judgement was considered and brought by the Committee of Privilege and Election in 1698. From these we can draw out the story of the ungentlemanly behaviour which occurred after the death of the young Sir William.[62] Unless otherwise stated, the tale which unfolds below is taken from the records in the *Journal of the House of Commons*.

The Protagonists

Sir William Williams, Bart (deceased since December 1696 and lately a Member of the House of Commons).

Dame Ellen Williams (his widow, and daughter of the Baron Hill estate in Anglesey).

Sir Bourchier Wrey of Tawstock in Devon (an infant).

John Barrington Esq. (Sir Bourchier Wrey's guardian).

John Evans, Gentleman (former steward to Sir William Williams of Faenol and co-executor of his Will).

Charles Allanson Esq. of the Middle Temple (an attorney-at-law and co-executor of Sir William's will).

Ellen Evans, widow.

Mr Arthur Owen of Orielton, Pembrokeshire and Bodeon, Anglesey (Member of the House of Commons and pretender to the heir-at-law of the Faenol estate).

Dame Jane Salusbury, widow of Sir John Salusbury, Bart., of the Lleweni estate in the Vale of Clwyd.

Although Owen undoubtedly supported his Meyrick neighbours' (Bodorgan, Anglesey) attempts to unseat the Bulkeleys (Baron Hill, Anglesey) from their 'political dictatorship of Anglesey,'[63] no reason has yet been ascertained why Owen should believe he was Pretender to the Heir at Law to the Faenol estate, or why Dame Jane Salusbury should claim to be co-heir to Sir William's estate with Arthur Owen ...

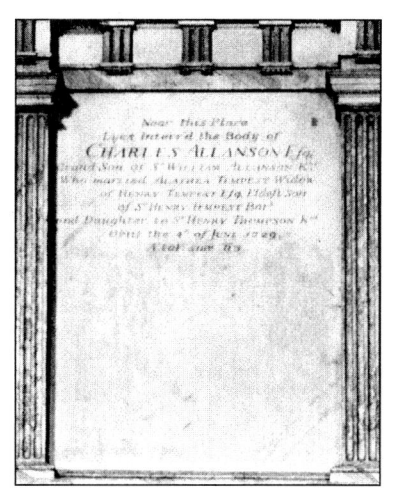

Memorial to Charles Allanson in Bangor Cathedral.

Sir William Williams, 6th Baronet of Faenol died on 23 December 1696, aged around thirty, one week after allegedly killing a man in a duel. The cause of his death is not known for sure, but it is entirely reasonable to speculate that he died of injuries sustained in that duel. His heir, as specified in the Will, was the infant Sir Bourchier Wrey, the son of Williams' friend the late elder Sir Bourchier Wrey.

It is alleged that the Wrey family had induced him to make such a will while he was drunk – 'in his cups' as they might have said. It is also rumoured that the reason he did not leave the Faenol estate to the Bulkeleys, to whom he might be said to have owed a great deal, was due to some argument, unresolved at the time of his death. This did not mean that the Bulkeleys had no further dealings with the Faenol estate; after all, the widowed Lady Williams was one of their own. After Sir William's death (which occurred in London) a 'Mr Bulkley' employed one William White to look after Sir William's personal estate on behalf of the executors of the Will, the estate's steward, John Evans, and Sir William's attorney, Charles Allanson, of the Middle Temple. In effect this meant that William White was engaged to reside at Faenol Old Hall to ensure that a male presence was kept there. While Sir William's widow, Dame Ellen would continue to oversee the organization of the house and household, the daily business of running an estate would mean that people would continue to call at the property and decisions which did not concern the steward would still need to be made and security would need to be maintained. Dame Ellen was herself attended by a female servant called Dorothy Davis. All four would later be called upon to give evidence on events which were about to unfold.

Christmas and New Year celebrations that year must have been rather overshadowed at Faenol with the death of the master of the household. While arrangements were made to transport Sir William's body back from London, the Faenol household was busy preparing for what must have been a sizeable funeral held at the cathedral church in Bangor where his body would be interred with those of his predecessors in the Faenol tomb. Perhaps extra or new plate and linen needed to be procured or prepared, as well as all the meat and drink necessary for the wake. Curiously the committee would later report that when 'Sir William Williams' Corpse [was] brought down into the Country, his Executors had not the liberty of Vaenoll House to lay it in; but made use of the Bishop of Bangor's House for that Purpose.' The troubles that would beset the estate would not begin until the spring, and we cannot imagine that the funeral would be delayed four months after Sir William's death, so the exact circumstances around this part of the pre-funeral arrangements must remain something of a mystery. One almost wonders, given that there are rumours of discord between Faenol and Baron Hill, whether his wife and her relatives would not allow the body back in the house. Surely though, decorum must have been maintained and, as a later document refers to meat and drink procured for the funeral, we can be certain that a wake at least was held in the house after the funeral.

We must hope that the following three months allowed Dame Ellen some peace, for in the following April (1697) Arthur Owen, MP, arrived at Faenol, backed up by armed men, including one William Wynn, who played an active role in the unfolding dramas. Owen claimed to be heir-at-law to the Faenol estate and intended to take what he saw as his by right.

It seems unlikely that the Faenol household had any warning of this incursion; otherwise we can be sure that armed men would have been waiting for Owen. As it was, Owen's band of men forcibly evicted William White and several other servants from the Hall. A petition in the January of 1698 alleged that there were fifty men present on this occasion, although of course we might allow for exaggeration borne of grievance with these figures. Owen's intention was not only to take control of the property but also the contents within it. The Committee of Privilege and Election reported that four trunks of papers and documents were removed from Faenol House by Owen's men, although John Barrington's original petition of April 1697 had claimed that three sacks worth of papers were taken along with a quantity of furniture. The fact that Dorothy Davis would later state that furniture was broken indicates that the intruders had orders to ransack the property and that documents were high on the agenda. As with any business, an important part of seizing control is without doubt to have access to the company records and Arthur Owen obviously cared little how much care was taken in looking for them. This removal of papers certainly accounts for the complete lack of any documents pertaining to this period amongst the Faenol papers. Four trunks, or even three sacks of papers, could easily encompass major land agreements and negotiations over that period, not to mention the day-to-day recording and minuting of business dealings, leases and tenancies, and the household accounts. Those documents which have survived to give us glimpses into the early history of the estate have done so in the archives of the other landed estates in the area, with which the Williams family of Faenol were intertwined through business and marriage.

The accounts of several witnesses of the breaking and entering of Faenol were also reported by the Committee. A servant, Dorothy Davis, had been out when Mr Owen and his men arrived. Upon her return she found Mr Owen and several others in the House 'and the Cabinet, Escritoire and Dressing-table in the Lady Williams' Chamber broke, which was not so when she went out.' This frightening experience and the facts as Dorothy related them were confirmed in a later petition to the House of Commons (4 February 1697) where Lady Williams herself complained of her chamber and closet being broken into. Furthermore, and as a great insult to the widow of one large estate owner and the daughter of another, Owen would not allow her her dower which was hers in terms of possessions, money and land, and which, as the widow of a wealthy estate owner, would have been considerable.

It sounds as though Dame Ellen had not been at home at this time of trouble, perhaps staying with friends or relatives, or at another residence elsewhere, possibly in London or Chester. This may have been just as well, as during the event itself Arthur Owen made sure that it was understood he was taking control of the property and, availed himself of whatever was on offer. Two further witnesses, John Parry and Sir William's former steward, John Evans, bore testimony to the fact that 'Mr Owen made use of all the Plate, Linen, and Meat and Drink, in the House, and particularly of what was provided for the Funeral of Sir William Williams.'

Owen did not just break in and take possession of the house at Faenol, he also wasted no time in making his presence felt within the grounds and in the wider estate. One witness, Edward Williams, reported that 'Mr Owen had caused to be cut down Thirteen Oaks, Nine Ashes; [and that] Twenty very small Walnut-trees were missing after Mr Owen had taken possession.' Nor did Owen stop there in his bid to show who was boss. The petition submitted to the House of Commons by John Barrington and John Evans in the April of 1697, on behalf of the infant Sir Bourchier Wrey, complains that Owen's men also turned the cattle from off the land farmed by the estate for its own purposes ('the demesne'). They then moved on to the properties of several of Sir William's tenants, turning the cattle out again if they refused to recognise Owen as their landlord. One tenant in particular, the widow

Ellen Evans, had her house broken into and her goods thrown out into the street. Furthermore, the men drove her cattle off her grounds and locked up her barns and cow houses. The plural here suggests that she was no smallholder, but the tenant of a sizeable property and the fact that John Barrington and John Evans had included her as co-petitioner may corroborate this. If she was an important tenant, or at least the widow of one, this may have earned her special treatment from Owen's enforcers.

The petitioners' grievances were compounded, they alleged, by the fact that Owen used his position as a member of parliament to threaten the local justices of the peace so that they dared not take action against him. Meanwhile, Owen continued to cut down and destroy the woodland on the Faenol estate and threatened to beat the devisees (by which was meant Barrington as guardian) and the Executors (John Evans and Charles Allanson) with their own weapons.

The House of Commons took a dim view of Arthur Owen using his privilege in this way and decreed that 'No Member of this House hath any Privilege in Cases of Breach of the Peace, or forcible Entries or forcible Detainers.'[64]

Arthur Owen was not a man to be put off by such rulings and continued to maintain a presence at Faenol. Meanwhile, feelings continued to run very high and in the September of 1697 Owen's man, William Wynne, on the road to Faenol, met the attorney Mr Allanson, and his man. The ensuing verbal altercation culminated in Allanson threatening Wynne with 'a Brace of Bullets in his Belly.'[65] Wynne would later give witness that he believed that Allanson would have done so too, if he had not been restrained by his man. It would have been interesting to know more about that day; did the two parties chance to meet, or was one or the other looking for trouble? Was Wynne similarly armed? We will see that later in the year John Evans, the former steward, was also to threaten Owen's men with a pistol – the stakes over land and privilege were high, and while there is no record in any of the reports of anyone actually being shot, there is no doubt that the ongoing dispute was attended by violence and disturbance. Allanson and Evans of course had a vested interest in the maintenance of the status quo with their former employer's will; they both gained financially from it and so their interests were best served by preventing Arthur Owen from gaining ground.

In light of this we should not be surprised to hear that Owen was not to enjoy 'peaceable possession' of the Faenol estate for too long. On 1 December 1697, Thomas Bulkeley,[66] Charles Allanson and Cadwaladar Wyn, led John and Hugh Evans and others to the house and forcibly ejected the occupants. Arthur Owen may have imagined that after eight months his heavy-handed tactics had won the day and was to complain bitterly that he had been menaced by the arrival of Bukleley and Allanson *et al*, and that they had also distrained his tenants and assaulted and wounded his agents and servants. Hugh Morgan, a reluctant witness called before the Committee of Privilege and Election, reported that he had heard that Mr Owen's servants were beaten by Hugh Evans. He further declared that Mr Owen had sent a warrant to him as Under-Sheriff for the apprehending of the said Hugh Evans. Hugh Evans had responded to this warrant by cocking his pistol against him and threatening to kill him, saying that Mr Owen was a rebel. Evans had further threatened to cut Owen's brother-in-law Sir William Williams' head 'as a calf's head'.[67] The reference to the calf's head is most likely to be a reference to the Calves Head Club who reputedly met on 30 January each year on the anniversary of the beheading of Charles I. Calves heads were served at a feast and 'anthems' sung. How much the general populace knew about this secret society is unclear, but it seems likely that the phrase was in current usuage as a term for beheading. In addition, the Calves Head Club was said to be composed of Whiggites and as the Faenol/Bulkeley party were Tories there was an added insult intended there.[68]

One might wonder what role the local authorities played in all this drama. In fact the gentlemen of the county *were* the authorities to all intents and purposes, and with no official, organised police force until the nineteenth century, it was the gentry in their roles as sheriffs and justices of the peace who were responsible for ensuring that the law of the land was upheld. Dramas between themselves were a tricky business therefore and while we should not see them as being above the law, they were playing for high stakes and, just as today, when people play for high stakes, physical force or the threat of violence, and bribery and corruption, are and were often the leverages applied to try to secure each party's preferred outcomes. The fact that this dispute ended up in the House of Commons indicates its serious nature.

The next protagonist to enter the picture is one Dame Jane Salusbury, claiming in a petition to the House to be co-heir with Arthur Owen of Sir William Williams' estate. She asserted in her petition that in December 1697 Owen had had 'peaceable possession of [the] Estate at Vaenoll' but that John Evans had obtruded on their possession on behalf of Sir Bourchier Wrey. This ejectment she maintained was obtained by force by Evans 'and many others' and was backed up by the Sheriff without Owen being able to put his case for the defence. She suggests that bribery and force were the key to this judgement by the Sheriff in favour of Evans/Wrey.

Whatever the circumstances, it appears that Hugh Morgan, the Under-Sheriff, had delivered possession of Faenol to a Mr Hughes, lessee for Sir Bourchier Wrey on 1 December 1697, as witnessed by one John Glynn. Glynn confessed however that he had been 'obliged to give the Under-Sheriff Twenty Guineas, and a Bond of [£]500 to [render] him harmless' – presumably meaning the bribe referred to by Dame Jane Salusbury.

By these January 1698 petitions, the House of Commons was obviously taking the issue seriously, or despairing of the feud being resolved, and each new petition was referred to the Committee of Privilege and Election with the request that they 'do examine the matter thereof; and report the same with their opinion therein to the House.'

Meanwhile the liberation of Faenol Hall on behalf of Sir Bourchier Wrey at the beginning of December would be short-lived. Less than a month later on 31 December, about thirty or forty people descended on Faenol on Owens' behalf at about five o'clock in the morning. In the pitch black of the midwinter morning John Parry lit a candle and went to investigate. As he pulled back the long iron bolt and opened the door, a stick was inserted in the gap to force the door open and Parry was thrown to the floorboards. The mob charged through the panelled hall room and up the two steps into the heart of the house. The silence of the morning was shattered by the clatter of boots on floorboards and lamps casting sinister jostling shadows as the occupants were manhandled from their beds and turned out into the cold and darkness of the New Year's Eve dawn. Having secured the property once more for Arthur Owen, the mob was despatched to turn the cattle loose again.

If Arthur Owen thought that matters were settled, he must have been aggrieved in Feburary 1698 when John Glynn and Mr Hughes arrived at Faenol demanding possession. On this occasion, Mr William Wynn and Thomas Davis stoutly kept possession for Mr Owen. Yet only a few weeks later the matter came to be resolved by the Committee of Privileges and Elections, which decreed that Arthur Owen had no rights in the case. This being supported by the House of Commons meant that the Wrey family faction, and the key players such as Charles Allanson and John Evans, continued to enjoy the rights over Faenol as Sir William Williams, 6th Baronet, had intended.

Chapter 8
Quieter times

Having been subsumed in the short term, firstly as a remote appendage of the estates of the Wreys of Tawstock[69] and thence as a permanent fixture into the extensive holdings of the Smiths/Assheton Smiths of Tedworth,[70] most of the eighteenth century was a fallow time for the Faenol demesne. Although the surviving documentary evidence is scant for this period, the estate surveys undertaken in the 1770s and 1790s suggest that for most of the eighteenth century Faenol's owners seem to have treated the estate as little more than a bank balance, rather than as a holding ripe for development.[71]

From the phase of the Wrey family ownership of the Faenol estate in the eighteenth century, there are enough papers surviving in the Faenol collection at Gwynedd Archives to show that the Wreys employed an agent to manage affairs up here. However, it may be that the turbulent events of the late 1690s had soured the connection for the Wrey family with the Faenol and they eventually leased the estate to attorney Charles Allanson for much less than it was apparently worth.[72] Despite this, issues connected with managing the estate and the ramifications of Sir William Williams' will forced themselves on the Wreys' attention whether they desired it or not. Documents such as a report commissioned by Thomas Smith in 1725 on matters at Faenol and various legal procedures brought by John Gore and John 'Speaker' Smith, also his sons Thomas and Henry Smith, against the Wrey family and Charles Allanson in the early eighteenth century show that the Smith family were taking a great deal of interest in their future Welsh lands well before they acceded to them.

Whether the Wreys ever lived in Faenol is unknown, but given their lack of interest over the next half century, it seems unlikely that they were ever more than visitors. Having said that, we do not know who, if anyone, lived at the Old Hall from the time of the events following Sir William's death in 1696 until Michaelmas 1785. At this date a surviving agent's account book records that a Mr William Jones, one of the estate's under-agents, was the tenant of the house and a certain amount of attendant land. By 1792, Mr Jones had been replaced as tenant by another under-agent, William Lloyd. The rent to both these men was £164 per annum – no small sum. However, William Lloyd at least came from a minor gentry family and as his wages as under-agent would not have anywhere near paid for his rent, we must assume that Mr Lloyd, and probably also Mr Jones, had some form of private or alternative form of income. Lloyd and his wife Eleanor probably remained at Faenol until his death in 1808, aged fifty-three.[73] Of their seven children it was their second child, Morgan Lloyd, who took over residence at the Old Hall, farming the land until the 1830s.

With the coming of the Speaker John Smith's descendants to the ownership of the Faenol estate in the 1750s, the quieter times receded into the past.[74] By the time that the Assheton Smiths had recovered from their new century celebrations in 1800, trade and industry had made their Welsh lands both prosperous and desirable through the slate held under its soil. A new, up to the minute fashionable and substantial country villa was completed at Faenol by 1795. Here the Thomas Assheton Smiths, father and son, could entertain the great and the good, and so the Old Hall found itself no longer the showpiece home, or even the second home, of the owners. The Assheton Smiths were very much focussed on Tedworth House in Hampshire as their ancestral seat and family home as it had been for two centuries. No longer a flagship to welcome and impress visitors, the Old Hall descended down the social scale through home of the estate under-agents to farmhouse. The formal label 'Home Farm' never seems to have been applied to the old property, although that was undoubtedly to be its main role for the next two hundred years.

Three decades later, Morgan Lloyd, farmer and tenant at the Old

Hall, a place that had been the Lloyd family home for at least forty years, found himself prey to the changing winds blown in by the new owner in the form of Thomas Assheton Smith junior. Tom Smith, as he was known, had waited many years in the shadow of his long-lived father. Now that he was free to make what changes he liked he instituted a great deal of radical change throughout all his properties in Hampshire, Cheshire and at Faenol. In 1831, a programme of work was begun at the Old Hall to revamp the structure of the building and improve the comforts for the occupants. Instead of hauling slates from Nant-y-Garth to the newly expanded Port Dinorwick, the slate wagons rumbled their way to the Old Hall and were expertly unloaded and stacked by the tough men who worked with these massive slates day in day out. Up on the roof, standing on the sixteenth and seventeenth century roof timbers with the casual ease borne of years of experience, the roofers manhandled the massive new 'King' and 'Empress' sized slates into position. Watching their progress, Morgan Lloyd would have seen a big difference in style as the tide of new slate spread across the peaks and valleys of the roof of his home. At 6" x 10" the original Tudor slates had been diminutive compared with the massive new slates which were replacing them.[75] The original slates were not all discarded however, with some being retained to be reused as packing around the edges and in the roof valleys. Dating their work, the master roofer scored his initials and the year into the torching (lime mortar) which sealed the underside of the slates.

Now that the house was watertight once more, stone workers arrived on site to replace some of the original stone window mullions with new stone, matching the arched mullioned design of the original. Others, being in a better state of repair, were retained to do service to the present day. The interior of the room inside the front door – known to the Williams family as the hall – was partitioned off with panelling to create a corridor leading from the front door to the centre of the house, affording the remaining room some probably badly needed relief from the drafts blowing in round the sixteenth-century door. Finally, to complete the renovations, an external door was added to the outside of the porch, no doubt with the same draft-excluding intention, as the remaining iron hinge brackets in the stone door jamb testify.

Whether Morgan Lloyd continued to reside in the house during these renovations is debateable. A house with its roof off is very much an open box and prey to the elements. But whether he toughed it out or not, his landlord, Thomas Smith, had new plans for the old property and the attendant farmland, and for the time being decided to offer the refurbished house as a home to the retiring cook from the new Faenol Hall, Betty Hughes, and her husband. The letter informing the estate's agent of this change of occupancy also stipulated that Lloyd must be found another farm if possible. The estate Letter Book does not record Morgan's thoughts on the subject!

Many Tudor gentry houses of this size owe their survival today to their useful solid construction and number of rooms, lending themselves admirably to the later accommodation of a farmer, his family and their household and outdoor staff as happened at Faenol Old Hall and nearby Glasgoed Hall near Bethel. Many more properties were not so fortunate and were knocked down or integrated into newer fashionable buildings as happened at neighbouring Plas Newydd and Penrhyn Castle. Cochwillan Hall, Thomas Wyn ap Willim's childhood home, served as a barn for many years before restoration work rescued it from complete dilapidation. The retention of Faenol Old Hall in the late 1700s probably has much to do with its location, tucked away behind a curving fifty-metre contour line with little view or pride of place. To the original locators of the site (probably long before Thomas Wyn ap Willim was born), this hidden setting was probably its greatest bonus. To Thomas Assheton Smith senior however, it was probably just one of its many drawbacks. Rather than razing it to the ground, he rode over the surrounding fields until he was satisfied with the location for his new villa – at the top of a slope where the view could be admired and where the visitor approaching up the drive, or the sportsman on his horse in the grounds could admire its sparkling white splendour. A tree barrier was planted to ensure that the Old Hall was screened from view.

Without the benefit of a census record for this early part of the nineteenth century it is hard to know whether Betty Hughes and her husband lived alone in the Old Hall, or whether it was generally being used as a residence for estate staff. It is not hard to imagine that a female servant may have been provided to help out – Tom Smith obviously took his obligations to key staff members seriously. Mr and Mrs Hughes may have lived in the Old Hall for the best part of a decade, living through such domestic dramas as the stormy night in 1831 which caused part of the wall surrounding the walled garden to collapse in theatrical fashion, breaking some of the plum trees that were growing in the orchard there.[76] However, by the time the inaugural official census was taken in north Wales in 1841 the Hugheses were no longer in residence. For a short while the tenancy of the Farm had been the domain of one Edward Roberts who, it is said, was a kind and well thought of person who settled at the Faenol after he got married. Unfortunately his wife died soon afterwards leaving him with a young daughter and in pining sadly for his wife, Edward's own health deteriorated. He arranged for his sister's son, Ellis James a farmer from Llanberis, to take over from him at the farm and to bring up his small daughter and in 1840, shortly after making these arrangements, the unhappy widower died himself.[77] A farm and its household do not run themselves and, at the age of 28 the young bachelor Ellis James presided here at the Faenol Farm House over a household of seven agricultural labourers and three female servants. It was not until 1850, after 'roaming this way and that in my quest for my life's partner', that Ellis married Jane Griffith, a

Ellis James. [Struan James-Robertson]

girl from Ederyn on Penllyn and in 1852 they had their first child Catherine, followed by a boy, Robert, in 1856. Ellis was a successful farmer, as yet untroubled by the Great Agricultural Depression that would dominate the later years of the nineteenth century. He was also a deeply religious man, inspired by a sermon he had once heard while staying with his uncle Edward at Faenol. In time he would become an elder at the nearby Y Graig Calvanistic Methodist chapel and as an educated man who could read and write he became secretary to the Arfon Methodist Monthly Meeting in 1846.

Jane James.
[Struan James-Robertson]

In 1853, on his fortieth birthday, Ellis James took stock of his life to date, writing in his diary:

> I moved from Tŷ Gwyn to Vaynol [Old Hall] in August 1840. For years I had been unhappy at Llanberis and knew that there were better things to do than roam the hills after sheep day after day, summer and winter, in all weathers. I was sometimes soaked to the skin and shivering cold, and there was no hope of improving my way of life, so when my uncle Edward Roberts died I moved to the Vaynol. Life there at the beginning was very hard and I can remember two occasions when I had less than five shillings to my name and no hope of a penny from any other source. I had always wanted a pleasant place to live – not great riches – but a nice home, a place where I could be of service to my Maker. I could hardly believe that I had been so blessed as to have had the Vaynol. Not one Sunday passed from the day I arrived

there to this day without a sermon being preached at the Vaynol and I trust it will still be the same to the end of my days.[78]

Despite some hard times, including years of drought like 1859 when the fields were parched, animals died of thirst and Ellis was compelled to sell most of his starving cattle, he was able by 1861 to proudly declare himself a 48 year old farmer of 350 acres to the census enumerator who visited the Old Hall. Ellis James' religion and vigorous nature kept him strong, and such was his feeling of independence from the establishment Anglicanism of his employer and landlord that he did not fear to invite Calvanistic Methodist preachers such as John Jones, from Llanynghenedl on Anglesey,[79] to stay with the family and their household of nine staff (comprising of agricultural labourers, dairy maids, cowmen and servants). During his time at the Farm at Faenol Ellis James kept Welsh language diaries, from which the excerpts above were taken, and which can be seen at the archives at Bangor University. These include the Faenol farm accounts and rent receipts.

Revd John Jones [Richard Evans]

While Ellis James had been building up his farming empire on the Faenol demesne, his nearest farming neighbour Daniel Roberts had been doing the same at the far end of Faenol Park, nearest the newly constructed Port Dinorwic. The Faenol peninsula was still very much a set of discrete farms as it had been since medieval times, albeit under the same ultimate ownership of the Assheton Smith family. Thirty-five-year-old Roberts, his wife Anne and their two young girls were already established at Bryn Adda farm when the first set of census enumerators came knocking in 1841. Bryn Adda house must have been a sizeable property, or else the twelve household and farm staff lived in exceedingly close quarters, occupying every nook and cranny of the old farmhouse. Daniel Roberts' household grew even larger over the next decade with the addition of three more children, and Ellen Williams, his daughters' governess. Roberts was also a religious man, and when not farming, was a lay preacher and the treasurer of the *Cyfarfod Misol* (Monthly Meeting), Arfon Presbytery for several decades. Like his neighbour his chosen faith was that of a Calvanistic Methodism, and doubtless discussions in front of the fire on winter evenings at Faenol and Bryn Adda roamed much wider than just their mutual farming interests.

Bryn Adda house was described at the turn of the nineteenth century as comprising of 'a dwelling house and stable under one roof slated and in bad repair, a shed lately built by lessee [Richard Jones] is a badly built shed in bad repair.'[80] Even if Daniel Roberts, who established himself on the 1861 census as a farmer of 200 acres and ten years later as a 'Gentleman and Landowner', had since seen to repairs and renovated the property, there can be no doubt that his neighbour Ellis James had the superior property and more land. Doubtless the Faenol Farm was a prize worth having.

Eventually, both Roberts' and James' luck ran out. The infant, George Duff Assheton Smith, inherited the Faenol estate at the end of the 1850s, his father Robert Duff, like Tom Smith before him, had made many changes, including beginning the building the of the park wall we know today, and the older and less workable parts of the demesne were replaced with modern new buildings and systems more suited to the needs of the day. Farming techniques and estate management were changing and perhaps there simply was not room for two sizeable farms with long term leases within the demesne, particularly

Medallion showing George Duff, issued to commemorate his twenty-first birthday

Faenol Old Hall, north front, c.1880. [Author's collection]

with the onset of the Great Depression. Seismic changes were afoot.

In 1869, Ellis James was asked to quit the Old Hall and to take over Ty'n Llwyn in Pentir. By 1871, he had been replaced at the Old Hall (or Vaynol Farm as it was then indisputably known), by a career farm steward, a Scotsman named John Reed. To employ their senior estate staff from out of the area was usual practice for any landed estate and Scotsmen were seen as particularly reliable. During his career, Reed had encountered a young lady from Norfolk named Susannah, whom he made his wife. House-hold staff in a big house like Faenol New Hall were discouraged from marrying, but doubtless a wife was entirely appropriate for these more independent senior members of the estate management; at the very least a wife would keep order in the farm household and supervise the indoor staff. Together with their son Joseph, the Reeds had moved from Scotland to Faenol, living at the farm with a much smaller staff; two local girls, one of whom kept house and the other in the dairy, and two brothers in their twenties who had moved down from Scotland with the Reeds to work as gardeners on the estate. Meanwhile Bryn Adda farmhouse had been demolished and a

William Lort
[Roma Lort Jones]

row of tenanted cottages and a larger property built in its stead. The estate surveys describe the Bryn Adda land as being 'in hand' by which was meant that it had been encompassed within the estate's home farm.[81]

Faenol Farm was now a part of the unified business with a manager in post, rather than a farmer who made it his home. As might be expected in these circumstances, John Reed's incumbency in the farm manager post did not endure. As a career man he moved to a bigger and better estate somewhere else and so, by 1881, a new and more mature face ran the farm at Faenol. The new occupants were James Kent, his wife Caroline and their twenty year old son Benjamin. George Duff Assheton Smith, the estate owner (known more usually by the name he was born with, George Duff) had grown up largely on the Isle of Wight, and James Kent himself hailed originally from the same island. As James and Caroline's son had been born in the county of Kent, we might presume that he also had been a career estate farm manager, originally farming on the Isle of Wight and perhaps being known to Duff, or his father, before he established himself at Faenol.

During the later decades of the nineteenth century, George Duff Assheton Smith's friend and private secretary lived at the Old Hall. The 1891 census shows this man William Lort, his children, butler, cook and housemaid living at the property. Earlier census returns had listed the house as 'Vaenol Farm House', but William Lort, or perhaps George, had re-christened it Vaynol Old Hall. William 'Beaver' Lort was an employee, but also a close personal friend of George Duff, or The Squire as he was known to the Lort family. The use of the Old Hall as a residence for this man and his family implies that the Old Hall was rising in status once more. Whether either of these two men were interested in its historical significance is lost to the winds of time. Antiquarianism was a popular Victorian interest and the historical aspects of old buildings took on a new significance at this latter end of Victoria's reign. As far as it is possible to tell from the photographs, it seems that the general architectural appearance of the Old Hall was reasonably unchanged in William Lort's day, despite, or because of, the structural 'tidy-up' it had received earlier in the century. From William Lort's diaries, kept while in the Arctic Ocean in George Duff's steam yacht *Pandora,* it seems that what both men really enjoyed was shooting animals. The trips in the yacht were so successful in this aspect that the old chapel opposite the old Hall was used as a museum to display the stuffed trophies of the Arctic trips. Whatever the views of the Squire or Beaver Lort on antiquarianism, the change of name from

A damaged and faded photograph of the interior of the ground floor hall room, Faenol Old Hall, during the time of William Lort's residence, c.1890. Behind the Victorian décor you can see the original seventeenth-century panelling. [Roma Lort Jones]

A damaged and faded photograph of the interior of the first floor room, Faenol Old Hall, which the Williams family used as their dining room. Photograph taken c.1890. The panelling in this room was of higher quality than that of the hall room below and featured William Williams, first baronet's Arms in the chimneypiece. [Roma Lort Jones]

the Farm House to Vaynol Old Hall demonstrates that the residence was felt to need a more formal title to reflect the status of its occupants. The importance of the Lort family at Faenol continued after William's death when his eldest son, Thomas Lort, became the head of the household at the Old Hall, as befitted his position as the estate's agent. After the Squire's death and the reins of the estate being taken over by his brother, Sir Charles Assheton Smith, the Lorts were offered another property and in 1905, they held a big sale of their possessions from the

Old Hall.[82] As a tenant, your certainty of renewal of contract held only as long as your star waxed strong with the person who had put you there. Come change of owner or change of business need and you were moved on to pastures new.

During the twentieth century the Old Hall was home to a variety of farm managers, their staff and other people who were connected in some way to the Faenol estate. I have been lucky enough to meet a number of these people during the few years that we were able to give guided tours of the Old Hall and I thank them for the memories and insights they have given me regarding living in this old property. My particular thanks go to Rachel (Ray) Williams who bravely lived there on her own during a period of work on the house during the 1960s and the late David Gladstone who lived there for many years with his family.

Faenol Old Hall is now once more, as it should be, the home of members of the family of the current estate owners. Much work has been done over the last few years to renovate and repair it, and importantly to reinstate it as a family home after a number of years of being empty. The newer late eighteenth-century hall is always going to appear to be the flagship, with its sparkling white stuccoed exterior and prominent position, but the Old Hall continues to be the historical nucleus, the nurturing womb of the whole enterprise. All else is window dressing.

Appendices

Original Documents from the early history of Faenol
Where it has not been possible to decipher the original wording the text has been annotated with [...]. Where there is a doubt as to the accuracy of the transcription, the word (or words) in doubt has been followed by [?].

1. Faenol Inventory, 1669

This inventory is a fascinating glimpse into the contents of Faenol (that house now known as Faenol Old Hall), its gatehouse and the ancillary buildings that supported the household in July 1669.

Sir Griffith Williams cannot have been more than around twenty-five years of age at his death in 1669 and it would seem likely that his demise had not been anticipated as it was then customary to make your will only when you felt your life was drawing to an end. The absence of a will for this young man supports the suggestion that his death came unexpectedly.

All wills had to be proved through the relevant probate court which, for north Wales, was the Consistory Court of Canterbury. All the other Williams owners of the Faenol had their wills recorded there and the fact that there was none for Griffith stands out as something to remark upon. As wills were transcribed into large books, one after another as they were presented, it is unlikely that his will was lost.

Fortunately, another function of the probate process was that of the probate inventory which was a list, compiled by the executors of the will (assuming there was one), in order to provide the probate registry with a list of everything (moveable goods and chattels) that the deceased owned so as to establish his personal wealth. This, it is believed, protected the executors from any person claiming dues from the deceased's personal estate that were more than it could afford. The probate inventories were not always filed with the wills and after three and a half centuries it is not always possible to track the inventories down. It would have been fascinating to have had inventories attached to all the wills, but sadly this was not to be. To date, only the 1669 inventory for Sir Griffith Williams had been traced.

It would have been interesting to have had a map of the layout of the buildings detailed in the inventory but no such document exists and it is therefore difficult to establish the location of more than the main rooms in the house in relation to the property today. Even so, our voyeuristic instincts take over as we read through the contents of the rooms, forming a mental picture of the house and how its occupants lived.

Inventories usually followed a set routine round the property starting with the first room through the main entrance and then progressing through the most important rooms, even if this means that the inventory-makers had to traipse up and down the stairs several times. This pattern was apparently followed to the letter at Faenol in 1669 with the officials starting their listing with the hall, the first room they would have come to over the door threshold, and then moving on to the parlour behind before heading upstairs to Griffith and Penelope's chamber and closet and then the dining room. The other chambers could have been either upstairs or downstairs and, except where it states that a room is over another or is part of the garrett [attic], it is impossible to know their exact locations. Interestingly, the children's nursery, where the infants William and Thomas slept, comes way down the list, being assessed after all the other chambers and just before the maids' chamber.

What was listed in the inventories was intended to be all the moveable goods and chattels (but not the land and buildings) belonging to the deceased – some inventories listed these all the way down to clothes, but others did not go quite into this level of detail. At Faenol the assessors seem to have been very interested in the bedding, which is detailed down to the last cushion and rug, but there is no mention of any clothes, weapons or personal items such as jewellery or books.

One theme which runs throughout the inventory is that of the age of some of the items – some described as old and others (e.g. fabric) as rotten. This tells us that, like any house lived in for several generations of the same family, some items had been around for a long time, sometimes demoted to less favoured rooms, whereas other, newer, items were intended to impress with their up-to-date designs and fashions. By 1669, Faenol was not a particularly modern building, but that did not mean that the mistress of the house did not covet the latest fabrics and styles and it is noticeable that a number of the chambers are denoted by their colour. Not all the rooms, especially in a house of this size, would have been 'such-a-body's' chamber and often the most impressive chambers were kept as guest rooms for visiting family, friends and dignitaries. So where we read of a valence trimmed with silk crulis lace in the chamber over the buttery, or a silk fringed valence in the purple chamber; rooms with looking glasses (mirrors), tables and chairs and fire places, we know we are peeking into accommo-dation designed to afford comfort to visitors worthy of the best that the house could offer.

The outbuildings and gatehouse also provided accommodation, but to less exalted, although no less useful individuals. These were the people who worked in and around the hall and the farm. Their bed-steads and coverings are described generally in terms of being old, but we should note that, in their generally unheated chambers, the staff seem to have been accorded no less than the Williams family in terms of the numbers of bed covers.

Some rooms are designated for particular people, giving us some understanding of the extended household. In the house itself we have the 'Maydes' chamber, and in the gatehouse we have the 'Butler's little Roome' and the chamber where 'often Williams ye Chaplayne Lodgeth'; there was no point in having a chapel of your own, if you did not have a chaplain to lead you in worship. This suggests that the chaplain was a frequent guest, but perhaps not one who was offered one of the better guest bedrooms in the house. A mysterious visitor, not identified by name, once stayed in one of the ground floor rooms of the gatehouse, leaving such a strong presence behind that the room continued to be called 'Shiambar y Captayne' (the Captain's Chamber) after his departure. We should not forget that this was a mere twenty years after the end of the Civil War and it may be that a captain had lodged with the family during those troubled times. This room had a certain amount of comfort, with a table, stools and a cupboard, but there was a room within the gatehouse which was better appointed still, and that was the 'Red

A reproduction seventeenth century bed showing a truckle bed beneath. Beds of course varied in standard and decoration and this is not an especially elaborate example.

Chamber'. This room, although the furnishings may not have been new, was served by a bed with curtains and a valance, a red cloth carpet and a looking glass, as well as a table and chairs. Visiting gentry might bring staff with them and it might be that this room was reserved for the manservant of some noble visitor, or perhaps a lady's maid, although she might be more likely perhaps to sleep on a truckle bed in the chamber in the house where her mistress slept, so as to be on hand.

One thing that unified everyone was the need to use the lavatory. The inventory gives us chapter and verse on how this was achieved, and as you might expect, the toilet facilities varied depending on your status. The larger chambers for family and guests were provided with 'Close-Stooles' – these were basically commodes disguised as chairs with a lift-up lid containing a pan that the maids would empty. The other rooms were not offered this convenience, however the list of pewter gives us a clue as to their facilities; a total of twenty pewter 'chamberpotts' are listed in the inventory.

The furnishings in the key reception rooms, as a modern estate agent would term them, give us more information about how the family used them, and the importance they accorded each room. The hall, just inside the front porch, was by 1669 a room, probably once the most important in the house, which was now a much more functional space. By that date people often had their servants eat their meals in the hall, and estate and legal business with staff, tenants and petty criminals was certainly a major function of such a room. Correspondingly, the furniture was very serviceable and plain – consisting of two tables, two forms [benches] (not even individual stools), a small table at the front and an old open cupboard. Not a room in which you would entertain a gentleman.

The parlour, through the door from the hall, was the place into higher-status guests would be invited. It would seem from the furniture that this was a more comfortable room, where you would spend the evening sitting on a horsehair-stuffed couch in front of the fire, perhaps with a jug of warm claret. Under your feet, the wide floorboards were covered with carpets (albeit old) – necessary for keeping down the draughts, and perhaps cooking smells, from the kitchen in the basement below. Interestingly, amongst the feature pieces of this room is something described as a 'decayed small glass' – not as you might think a damaged drinking vessel or even a mirror. It is believed that this might be a clock, and the only clock in the house if the inventory is accurate. Furthermore, the walls of this room, decorated in the fashion of the time with white plaster, bore the only two paintings in the house. What, or who, these portrayed is not recorded. Unfortunately no portraits of the Williams family of Faenol have survived and it is not inconceivable that these may have been portraits of Griffith's grand-father Sir William and his second wife Dorothy, commissioned at the time of his purchase of the baronetcy.

One of the most expensively furnished rooms in the house was the 'Dyneing Roome' which, unlike our dining rooms today, was located upstairs. This was somewhere only the great and the good were entertained and was located in the room next to Sir Griffith and Lady Penelope's chamber. We know that in the 1620s, Sir William had commissioned the oak panelling which covered the walls of the dining room and the stylish oak chimney piece which was the central feature of the room, advertised the lineage of the family and his baronetcy. This, however, was not considered a moveable item by the inventory-makers (although people did move things like floor boards if they moved house) and therefore does not make it into the recorded details. In fact if it had not been for Roma Lort Jones' old photographs of the house, we would not have known that this chimney piece ever existed as it was removed from the property some time during the early twentieth century.

The dining room is without doubt one of the largest rooms in the house and has a large stone mullion and transom window letting in plenty of light.

It needed to be large as it contained a great deal of good quality furniture. The inventory shows that the floor was carpeted with a 'great Turkie Carpett' as well as a smaller carpet. Turkish carpets, with their bright colours and deep velvety pile, had been imported to British shores from Asia Minor since the sixteenth century and, without doubt, this was a prestigious and expensive item. But the spending had not ceased there: twenty-eight 'Turkie work chairs'* were provided for the seating of a considerable number of guests. When light was poor, Lady Williams did not rely on candles alone, she also had use of two large sconces** on the walls, which no doubt reflected light well on to the silver flagons with their ornate lids and handles for serving wine, the 'great [silver] Salt Seller' and the silver spoons and individual silver trencher salt cellars*** which glittered on the damask table cloths and napkins with which the tables were laid for fine dining.

This brings us to the tables themselves, the four main tables are described as 'Sleight Spaynish Tables'. 'Sleight' might be read as 'slight' but this is unlikely as four tables that could sit twenty-eight people were unlikely to be of modest or small size. The word is more likely to be an inventive spelling for slate. Slate was quarried on a modest scale for domestic and even export markets from the mountains in seventeenth century Caernarfonshire, however the word 'Spanish' throws a spanner into that train of thought. Does this mean that the Williams family had imported slate (or perhaps slate-topped) tables from Spain? It is entirely possible, as almost any European luxury could be brought by ship to Bangor, Caernarfon or Beaumaris and perhaps they would see more kudos in an imported item than something that was locally made. The alternative way of looking at this is that they were slate (or slate-topped) tables made in a Spanish design, but perhaps made by a local craftsman rather than a Spanish one.

Those readers with children may note the lack of children-centred items on the inventory, which is all the more intriguing when we consider how much

---

* Turkie-work, was a form of knotted embroidery used for upholstery in imitation of the fashionable Turkish carpets and no doubt colours had been chosen to match those in the carpet below the well-shod feet of the diners.

** Sconces were candle holders.

*** Trencher salt cellars must therefore have held the salt for guests not seated near the 'great salt sellars' a large and expensive item.

paraphernalia surrounds babies and children today. The children's room 'The Nurserie' mostly contains the same furniture as the adult rooms with the only reference to a plaything being the 'toye beds'. Perhaps smaller toys were not considered to be worthy of inclusion on the list, but it seems strange that there is no mention of a crib until we remember that babies from wealthy families were often sent to live with wet nurses until they were weaned. However, on closer inspection of the items in Sir Griffith and his lady's Chamber, we do see one 'little couch Bedstid' and it may have been that this was a small bed for a toddler, too young to sleep apart from his parents. Seventeenth century children were expected to behave like small adults, and were certainly dressed as such. Poorer children toiled to earn money alongside their parents, and while their gentry contemporaries were likely to have more play time, their toys, which might have included hobby- or rocking-horses or toy bows and arrows, reflected adult pursuits and skills which the boys at least would be expected to perfect in young adulthood. Childhood as we see it as a carefree time to play only came along centuries later and toys as such were not widely available. Teddy bears and dolls' houses were all playthings of the future and perhaps the term nursery was just to denote that it was the children's chamber and might not have contained anything that we would consider very childlike.

As we move through the inventory, past the Nurserie and the Maydes chamber, we enter into the 'downstairs' world of Faenol Old Hall. Here, in fact, the world of the staff probably was largely downstairs due to the sloping nature of the site allowing a basement with windows, although domestic functions in the seventeenth century were not quite so separated and unseen as they became in the eighteenth and nineteenth centuries where houses were built with hidden back staircases so that staff could move around the house unseen. The Buttery for instance, was the place where the Butler kept and prepared the drink for mealtimes – we can see that amongst the items listed there is a Cistern; a vital piece of equipment for (as it says) keeping the silver flagons in to keep the wine or ale cool. Traditionally, the Buttery and the Pantry (where bread and dry goods would have been stored) would have been two small, cool dry rooms located at the end of the Great Hall, accessed by either one or two doors. Although the household at Faenol no longer used the Great Hall (now termed simply 'the hall') for the formal dining occasions that it would have initially when Thomas Wyn ap Willim first created a home for himself there, it is likely that these two rooms would have remained in their ground floor location for those very same reasons of relative dryness and convenience for the Butler. Access to the dining room came via the staircase which ascends through the middle of the house and the Buttery and the Pantry were located near the stairs on the ground floor.

Downstairs below the parlour, and sharing the chimney stack with the parlour fireplace, was the Chitchin [kitchen] and the large fireplace where cooking was done. As you read through the contents of this domestic heart of the downstairs world, where the male cook presided, and through the inventories of the other domestic rooms and outbuildings – beer cellars, brewhouse, dairyhouse and cheese room, and slaughter house – you will begin to see just how self sufficient households such as this really were. No popping to the supermarket for them! And it was not just food, for if you look carefully, you can find other evidence of home production of products such as '2 great wheels for wool' and a 'parcel of hempen yarn', a 'parcel of Cloth for Blanketts' and 'whooles' stored throughout the buildings.

Finally, the inventory gets around to that other important institution for any landed estate; the Home Farm. This term is a later invention, and serves to conjour up images in the modern mind of vast Victorian 'model' farms and the 'Norfolk Four Course Rotation System' method of rotating ones crops. The model farm with its synchronised layout was as yet in the future and the scientific approach towards farming which was so promoted from the 18th

A reproduction sixteenth century bread oven.

century was by no means yet widely practised. Even so, Faenol's farm was without doubt a serious and modern concern, evidenced by the sheer size of the operation as listed in the inventory. In addition, it was blessed with several wheeled carts; '2 Great Carts [and] 3 smale Trolls' – troll carts being a narrow type of horse drawn cart. Most seventeenth century farmers would not have had the benefit of one wheeled cart, let alone five.

The final key piece that should be brought to the reader's attention is something that it would be easy to miss and which was stored in the Upper Stable – this was the Rolls Royce of the day; a 'Coach and Harnesse'. Here we get to the nub of the importance of the establishment; not only did they drink and eat from silver dining-ware, not only did they have heated bedrooms and a great Turkie carpet – the Faenol family were able to travel in the comfort and style of the gentry class in their own coach. To be sure, seventeenth century coaches were unsprung and wooden-wheeled, but in cold and unpleasant weather being seated inside with cushions to your back, rugs round your knees and a heated pan at your feet must have certainly beat travelling any distance by horseback.

A reproduction sixteenth century kitchen showing pots etc used by the cook. Fragments of brown-glazed pots like these have been found in the garden at Faenol Old Hall.

116 The Origins of the Faenol Estate

This inventory shows, on a practical level, exactly what it was like to live on a North Walian gentry establishment in the mid-late seventeenth century. Faenol was a key player on the county stage by this time, and the evidence of their wealth through land rents, official positions and business dealings is evident in this fascinating document.

A True and good fact Inventory of all Ye Householde Stuffe Goods Cattle and Chattle of Sir Griffith Williams of Vaynol Barronett, lately deceased taken ye Eight day of July Anno Dom 1669 Before Rich. Griffith Esq., William Williams, William Arthur, John Evance and John Owen Gent, Nominated and Appoynted to apprayse the same.

In ye Hall
Imprimis Two Tables, two formes and smale Table in the front and one ould open cupboard all valued att £1 15s 0d

In ye Parlour
Eight Chayres four Stooles one smael one 2 Tables one couch 2 ould carpetts 2 leather covers one Grate and Irons fire shovell Tongs and a payre of Bellowes and a decayed small glass with a payre of Tables 2 pictures all valued att £5

In Sir Griffith and his lady their Chamber
The Bedstid with flaxen Curtaynes and valence lynd with Callico. One ffeatherbed one Boulster 2 Pillows 2 Bolanketts one quilt counterpant one little couch Bedstid ffeatherbed and Boulster one blankett and coverlit one cabbanett one looking Glasse one small square Cupboard Table 10 Chayres and warming Pann, And irons framed with brass, Fflanen Hung about ye Roome and an oulde Clofe-Stoole valued att £10

In the Clossett thereto adjoyning
some few Glasse Bottles, Glasses and a [celler?] for smale Bottles all valued att £1

In the dyneing Roome
28 Turkie work chayres, one great Turkie Carpett and a smale one [...] A Brass and Iron, fire shovell and Tongs 2 large Skonshes 4 Sleight Spaynish Tables and a smale syde Table all valued att £11

In the Porch-Chaymber
One halfe Tester Bedstid ffeatherbed Boulster Blankett and a counterpane.

4 peirs of ould silk curtaynes and valence 6 lowe chayres covered with
fflanon and a Rotten flannon hung about ye Room all valued att £3

In ye White Chamber
The Bedstead with wrought Curtaynes and valence one ffeatherbed
boulster 2 Pillowes 2 Blanketts & a Coverlid. One couch Bedstead ffeather
Bed Boulster and blankett, & an ould one. Twelve wrought Chayres, one
little square Table, 2 stands for Basons, one looking Glass and Clofstools.
One payre of indirons ffireshovels & tongs all valued att £10

In the Purple Chamber
One Bedstead Curtains & valence trim'd with silk ffringe lyn'd with [...]
One ffeatherBed Boulster 2 Pillows one Blankett and a silk counterpane.
Twelve Chayres one little square Table with drawers one looking glasse 2
stands for basins one [....] indirons fireshovell and Tongs and Clofstools
and the Roome hung with Rome Cloth all valued att £12

In the [Clay?] Chamber
One Bedstid with ould silk curtaynes and valence one ffeatherbed boulster
2 pillows and blankett one coverlid. 4 Chayres and four Stooles one
fireshovell and tongs, one looking Glass and a clofe stoole
[...] £5

In the Passage Chamber
One Table, one press, 2 chests, one Trunk 2 Boxes a chayre, a joynt-stole
Warming pan and a payre of Tongs all valued att £2

In the Chamber above ye Buttery
One Bedstid Curtaynes and Valence Trim'd with ffringe of Silk Crulis Lace.
2 ffeatherBeds and Boulsters. 2 pillowes 3 Blanketts and Counterpane 6
Chayres 2 Stooles, smale grate fireshovel & tongs, one smale square Table
and 2 Looking Glasses, with KidderMaster hung around ye Roome, all
valued att £6 10s

In the Nurserie
One Bedstead and halfe a Testerbed 2 Featherbeds 2 Boulsters, 3 Blanketts
2 coverlidds, one little Square Table 2 ould Chayres curtaynes and valence
toye beds and a payre of Tongs all valued att £5

In ye Maydes chamber
2 ould Bedsteads 2 ffeatherBeds 2 Boulsters, 3 Blanketts 2 old coverlidds
one ould chest all valued att £2 10s

Part of the first page of the inventory of the goods of Sir Griffith Williams, 1669. [B 1668-59 I]

Part of the first page of the inventory of the goods of Sir Griffith Williams, 1669. [B 1668-59 I)

In ye Passage belowe and 2 Passage above
2 Cupboards and a Chayre in the Passage above one little square table and in the third 2 Trunks and a deale Box all valued att £1 15s

In the upper Garratt
2 ffeather beds one quilt Bed 4 Pillowes a dozen Blanketts one ould Rugg 7 old Trunks 3 old Chayres, 2 Chayres without covering. A parcell of Cloth for Blanketts, a parcel of hempen yarn, a parcell of [...] And whooles. All valued att £6

In ye outward Buttery
One Table one forme and an old chayre valued att 10s

In ye inner Buttery
One Table and Chayre 2 formes, one old chest, one old Trunk one Cistern for fflagons all valued att £3 10s

In ye Pantry
One Table 3 old chests valued at 10s

In ye lower Celler
20 Casks mosts of them Empty valued att £5

In ye Strong Beere Celler
14 Hogsheads valued att £5

In ye Chitchin
2 Racks 3 Spitts 2 dripping pans 3 payre of Potts-Hookes and one salt tubb. Chest, Cleaver chopping. The gridiron, fireshovell, Tongs, firestone, Beefe axe, fireplace, fflesh ffork all valued att £1
9 Brass Potts valued att £7
six smale panns and 4 smale skilletts valued att £1 10s
one great panne valued att £2 10s

In the Brewhouse
One Coombe 2 slatts [?] one Cookeing-Tubb 3 Pailes one little Tubb 3 old Barells one Tubb more one payre of slings to carrie Beere and a Funnell all valued att   £2 10s

In ye loft above the Brewhouse
One old Bedstead one ould featherbed, Boulster and an old blankett valued att £1

One Led Pann under the pump valued att £1

Pewter
71 dishes great and smale 19 sawcers
3 pastey Plates one Bason 8 syd plates 9 Trencher Plates, 3 [?]
of plate one ffish plate 6 Butter Plates 15 fflagons great and smale 20
chamberpotts one Bedpan 4 Stoole pans one smale Bason one porringer
21 candlstick and one still cover all valued att £20 11s
4 ould brass candlsticks 7s

Silver Plate
Twenty flagons [indecipherable] and cupp with a cover
a great Salt Seller 5 porringers another Salt Seller one Tankard, 3
Tumblers 6 Trencher salt sellers one Great Bolleigpott with a cover
32 spoones 2 Salvers 2 Gilt Cupps with covers all weighing 429 ouns and
1/2 all valued att £96 12s 09d

In ye dery-house
20 panns one great the others smale and a smale pott all valued att
£3 5s

An oulde Table, one Kniding Tubb, 2 old formes, one ould Trivett an Iron
fire fork, 9 ffleeches of Baccon, one Barell, one Churne, 7 Tubbs, 10 pales,
one great Tubb more, A great Leaden Cooler for milk in a frame, a dozen
noggins, 3 Cheese slats and 4 pitchers all valued att £5

In ye Cheese Roome
40 Cheeses, one Barell of Butters full 2 emptie Barells open, one Tubb,
one old Churne 2 ... cakes of Tallowe; one parcell of fflaxs 2 dressers (?)
and shelvs (?) (or shelds?) all valued att £7
27 ould Cheeses valued att £1 10s

In ye Slaughter house
3 Bracks and an old Chayre valued at 5s

In ye Chamber where Robert Parry Lyes
One Bedstead, a ffeatherbed, Boulster – very old, 3 blancketts, Coverlid,
smale table and a Chest all valued att £1 10s
In a smaler Roome where the old steward lay
Halfe Tester bedstead, ffeatherbed, Boulster 2 Blancketts one ould
Coverlid all valued att £1 10s

In the Gate House
Imprimis In the 2 lower Roome att ye first Entrance, In one of them 4 bedstids one ffeather bed 3 fflock beds, 6 blanketts, 4 Boulsters, one Rugg and 2 great wheeles for wooll(?) and in the other Chamber opposite to it, 3 Bedsteads that are very ould, 4 blanketts, 2 fflock 3 bolsters 3 ould Coverlids, A leaden Trou..h [?] for candles, one old Bullan (?) all valued att £4 10s

In ye Ground Chamber called Shiambar y Captayne
One half Tester bedstid [...] featherbed Boulster and one pillowe 3 Blanketts and a Coverlidd one Smale Round Table one Syd Cupboard and Chayre and stooles all valued att £2 10s

In ye Chamber above where often Williams ye Chaplayne Lodgeth
One Bedstid with Curtaynes, ffeatherbed, boulster, Pillowe, 3 blancketts and Coverlid, 4 chayres and a smale Table all valued att £2 10s

In ye Red Chamber
One Bedstid with ould fflanen Curtaynes and Valence, one ffeather Bed boulster 3 blancketts and a coverlid, 6 Chayres, coach smale square Table with Red Cloth carpett and a Looking Glass valued att £6

In ye Midle Chamber above ye Gate
One Bedsteed one Coverlidd, fflanen Curtaynes and valence, 2 old Chayres and one [...] cupboard all valued att £4

In ye next Roome to it
One Bedsted and a Trucklebed, one canopiebed 2 ffeatherbeds, one fflockbed, 2 boulsters, 4 blancketts 2 coverlids and one Rugg, old fflanen Curtaynes and valence and an ould Couch all valued att £4 5s

In ye Butler's little Roome
One ffeather-bed and one boulster 2 Blancketts 2 Chayres and a stoole Valued att £1

In ye Roome above it
One bedsteed with old Curtaynes, one ffeatherbed boulster 2 blanketts and a Coverlid and one old stoole an old candlstick. Valued att £1

In ye upper Garratt
5 Chayres and seven Stooles 4 blancketts one boulster and a black jack [?] and six [?] wheeles [?] and a table valued att £7 10s

In ye Inner Garratt
A parcell of wooll valued att £15
And a parcell of ffeathers valued att £1

In ye loft over ye Lower stable where ye Groome styes
2 smale Bedsteeds 2 fflockbeds 2 Boulsters 5 Blancketts, one ould Chest all valued att 15s

In ye Lower Stable
5 Sadles 5 Bridles and a pillion £1

In ye Upper stable
One little Bedsteed ffeatherbed and Boulster 2 Blancketts and coverlidd. One smale Table and litle Chest to keepe Oates valued att £1 5s

Coach and Harnesse valued att £11

In ye Granarie above the Upper Stable
A parcell of wheat valued att £4 16s
One dozen of Oake Boards valued att 12s
12 old forks (?) (sacks?) valued att 15s

All Matterialls for Winnowing
Old sheetes, Measuring [?] Shovells, sifs, [...] valued att 7s

In ye lower Granary
A parcell of Mault valued att £7
2 chests wherof one with a quantity of meal, one Jubb and some inconsiderable things valued att £2 10s

In ye litle Stone house and without
All the Impliments of Husbandry
2 Great Carts 3 smale Trolls and all other here belonging theronto is valued att £22

In Tu Wilach where ye Hynes doe lodge
4 smale bedsteads 9 blancketts and 4 Boulsters valued att £7
2 payre of scales and sevrall weights thereunto belonging the Iron [...] and cordes all valued att 10s

The Lynens
All the damasque, dyaper all ye Napery and other New and Old Table Clothes Sheets both within and without is valued att £50

Six dozen of wooden Trenchers att 5s

The horses and Mares both in stable and outhouse
25 rig, 18 horses, 7 Mares att £1 10s a piece amounts to £37 10s

Bay Penllech and the ould Gray Gelding valued att £7

Oxen
20 oxen valued att £7 a payre amounts to £70
16 oxen valued att [smudged] [...] a yoak amounts to £44

Coach-horses and Mares
4 Cows, 2 Mares and 2 Geldings valued att £24

Milck Kyne
37 and a Bull amounting to 49s a piece amounts to £76

Sheepe
709 Sheepe and lambs of all sorts in Maynol Bangor, Llanberis, Llanddeiniolen, Llanbair and Hirdrefaig(?) is valued at £134 12s 6d

Llanberis
18 heifers and a bull 3 and 4 years old apraysed to £1 13s and 4d a piece comes to £18 6s 8d
3 heiffers 2 year old att £1 6s 8d a piece valued att £4
2 splayed Heifers 4 year old appraised at £2 5s a piece comes to £4 10s
7 steers 4 year old appraysed at £2 a piece comes to £14
11 steers 3 year old appraysed at £1 7s a piece comes to £14 17s

At Hirdrefaig
11 oxen, 22 Milkskyne and Calfes and a Bull, 5 steers 3 year old, 2 steers and a Heffer of 2 year old, 6 Heffers and a steer of 3 year old all valued att £110

Household stuff there
6 old Blancketts, 2 payre of sheetes, 2 old Boulsters, 3 fferkins full of Butter and one with some in't, other 2 empty, another with a litle quantity of old Butter, 4 Cheese slatt, 3 smale [indecipherable] 2 [indecipherable] ould and the other new, 2 [indecipherable] 4 Shens [?], 2 Pitchers, 2 pales ¹/₂d

of Noggins a wooden Boule and a great Noggin and a Leaden pan to coole ye Milk all valued att £2

The old and new Hey and all the Corne at Hirdrefaig deducting therout £51 rent for the farme for the year is valued att £22

All the Corns at Boltandreg valued att £10

Hoggs, swynes and Poultry att Vaynol valued att £6

Att Bryn Adda milstons valued att £4

Debts due by Judgnts as the rest and damages amounts to £116 14s 9d

Arrears of Rents due upon Tenants in the severall parishes of Bangor, Penttir, Llandeiniolen, Llanberis, Llanfair and Llanllyfni amounts to £539 5s 2d

The sum total of the whole Inventory is 1656 pounds-6s-10d
[signed by]
    Rich Griffith
    Will Williams
    Will Arthur
    John Evance
    John Owen

Glossary of terms used in the Inventory
Bedstid/steed – bedstead – the framework of the bed
Black Jack – a lead weight used in mining / also a leather cup
Close-stoole – commode, also used as ordinary seating, and were sometimes equipped with cushions
Coverlidd - coverlet
Ffeatherbed – feather mattress
Fferkin – small cask for liquid, fish or butter, originally quarter of a barrel
Fflannon – early spelling of flannel – from the Welsh gwlanen meaning a woollen article
Fflockbed – flock tuft particle of wool or cotton used for stuffing beds, cushions etc.

Half Testerbed – A canopy over the head end of the bed – rather like half a four-poster bed

Hine/Hyne – a farm hand

Hogshead – a measure of beer

Indirons – more commonly spelt 'andirons' – they were a metal item used to support burning logs in a fireplace

Jubb – a vessel for ale or wine

Kniding tub – kneading tub

Milck Kyne – Kyne is an archaic plural of cow, therefore milk cows

Noggin – something for measuring liquids

Ouns – ounce

Porringer – a small dish, may have a handle

Press – a chest of drawers with a press on top to keep linen flat

Rig – like a gelding

Rome cloth – possibly imported cloth (maybe a purple colour??)

Slatts – possibly wooden slats left over from the coopering process of making barrels and other tubs used in the brewing process

Sleight – slate

Trencher – a wooden or silver platter from which food was served

Trolls – narrow horse drawn carts.

Trucklebed – a small bed which was usually rolled under the main bed out of the way except when in use.

2. The Last Will and Testament of Thomas Willims of Vaynol, 1592

In the name of god amen The twentie nineth daie of Aprill in the yeare of our lorde God a thousand five hundrethe ninetie twoe in the thirtie fourth yeare of the reigne of our Sovereigne Ladie Elizabeth by the grace of God Queene of England Ffrance and Ireland defender of the faith. I Thomas Willims otherwise called Thomas Win ap Willim of the parish of Bangor in the countie of Carnarvon beinge weake in bodie but of whole and perfecte memorie doe make my testamente contayninge thearein my laste will in manner and forme followinge.

Ffirste I commende my soule to the memorie of the Lorde God Almightie my creator and redeemer and my bodie to be buried in the cathedrall churche of Bangor and [...] and [...] maie be to the place where Jaine my wieffe was buried.

Item I give and bequeathe towards the reparations of the cathedrall churche of Bangor six shillinges and eighte pence. Item I bequeath towards the reparation of the parish church of Llanideniolen ffive shillinges. And offer five shillinges towards the reparations of the churche of Llan Tegai. Item to the reparation of the churche of Llanperis ffive shillinges.

Item I doe give devise and bequeathe to Simon Willims my younger sonn all the mortgaged landes tenanmentes followinge. Imprimis viz All the landes wich I had and purchased of Willim Griffith ap Alis ap Evans deceased or of his son. Item all the landes wich I had and purchased of Richard ap Willim Lloide deceased or of his sonn or of his brother.

Item all the landes wich I holde in mortgage of Richard ap Willim Roland the [...]. And incase the saide landes be redeemed then I give to the saide Simon Wms the somm of ffortie pundes of monie wich I laide out uppon the same. Item certaine other landes by me purchased within the comout of [...] in the towneship of Bodsais called Cwenn y Sayson.

Item the moitie of Elen Lewes tenemente by me purchased of Fred Baylie of Nanffrancon. Item one other tenemente of mine nowe in the occupation of Richarde Ffoxwiste the carrier. And one other tenemente of mine in the countie of Anglesey now in the occupation of Griffith ap Willim. To have and to holde all and everie the saide severall verified promises to the aforesaid Simon Willims my sonn, and to the heires made of his bodie carefullie begotten the remainder thereof in defaulte of [...] to be and remaine to my righte heires forever.

Item I give devise and bequeathe all my right claime title and intereste of and in the township of ...ke to my saide sonn Simon Williams. And my further will is that Willim Williams my eldeste sonn shall passe over onto the same Simon Willims all manner of righte and intereste that hath in him to doe of and in the saide Towneship without fraud or robbery.

To have and to hold unto the same Simon Willims his exequitore and assignees duringe all the yeare thereuppon yeat to come [...] that he the sonn Simon Willims shall and will in like manner release and surrender unto the said Willim Willims my eldeste sonn at all times uppon his request all further intereste subsequente as is in him of and in Dinorwick and Bodelog in the [...]. And the said Willim Willims shall require the same by his counsell lerned S. [...] and the saide Simon Willims shall have nothinge to doe with the one nor the said Willim Willims have anythinge to doe with the other and I doe repose in them in y Beriall coufideur [?] if I happen not to live to see the same performed between them myself.

Item whereas [...] of late depended in the marches of Wales between me and my Nephewe Willim Willims of Cochwillan esquire for the sum of five hundred marks of monie to me due and paiable at days longe paste by [...] in consideration of a marriage had between my sonn and his daughter wich bindes [...] letter in the custodie of Robert Win esquire and to him devised as of [...] to be kepte till the marriage weare [?] solemnized. The same monie I leave to my exequitor as due and charged uppon my saide Nephewe. If I my selfe doe not live to see out the matter [...] by this my saide testament that my saide Nephew the daie of ye sealing of the saide bondes did also undertake to me in the church of Conwey for the more summ of one hundred markes, the same also being firste promised and agreed uppon before ME [...] Win in a [...] had [...] the saide marriage and that with [...], that is the [...] of the Cwnis [?] woold not paie me the said sum for and in consideration of a [...] that was due uppon them, that then he woold paie it him selfe. I doe further certifie and devise that Robert Win the same daie of the sealinge of the saide bondes at Conwey and also at the said [...] before in Maurice Win his brother did also faithfullie promise and undertake to [...] for the paimente of one hundred marke monie for his parte towardes the saide marriage wich I also leave as due and charged uppon him as I hope he will not denie. This whole summ of ffour hundred marke to me due and paiable as aforsaid for the saide consideration I leave to be levied by my exequitor at his pleasure by himself of the parties and in further course where his remedie beste liethe if I doe not live to see out the matter my selff.

Item I give and bequeathe to the first daughters of [...] ap Owen ap Meirick beinge my daughters children the summ of twenty pounds of currente monie of England [...]. Tenn ound a peece towards either of their prefermente in marriage.

Item I give and bequeath to my daughter Katherine in [...] of my promise made in furnishinge of her wife apparell the summ of twenty markes of currente Englishe monie and one peere of plate of Silver in token of my remeberance of her, beinge of the cuppes whereof I have hidd [?] in a [...].

Item my will is that Morgan ap Jenn ap Meraild [?] my Servannt shall have and devise the tenemente wherein he nowe dwelles for terme of his lieff rente free. Item my will is that the said Morgan shall have meate and drinke duringe his lieff as he nowe hath and duringe such a time as he is contente to come for it. To whome also I give a summ of fortie shillinges of currente money towardes his findings.

Item I give and bequeathe to my cosen John Morgan of Beamaris a cowe and a calfe and of the twenty shillinges he dothe owe me I doe forgive yt him. Item my will is that Richarde Morgan my foster brother his wieffe and his sonn shall have and devise the tenement wheare in theie dwell, yealdinge and plinage for the same suche rente, profits and termes as he was wantes to doe.

Item I doe give and bequeathe to the said Simon Willims eighte oxen with the ploughe and the ploughe irons and other [...] belonging [...] theareunto. Also twenty four milch kine with their calves and a bull to followe them. Also further beaste of seven and four yeares old. A mare and twoe ffillies beinge in saide y park. A graie [...] Mare in my stable and [...] sheepe.

Item I give and bequeathe to the saide Simon Willims twoe featherbedd and twoe Coverlett remaininge in my house at Vaynoll. Item to him more one goblet of silver wich I had of Harrie Robbins, Six silver spoones wich I bought of John Lewes of [...]. Item a brasenn morter and pestle wich I bought of Ellen Gruffithe widdow and a bedstead remayninge in my chamber at Bangor in the custodie of Thomas Ffletcher.

Item I give and bequeathe to the same Simon Willims the sum of one hundreth poundes of currente money of England. Item I give and bequeathe to my daughter Elen Owen the late wieffe of Lewes ap Owen [...] towarde her second performense in marriage the summ of five hundrethe marke of currente monie of England.

Item I give to Evan Thomas of Coyde y parke twelve sheepe.

Item I doe make [...] and constitute my sonn Willim Willims, otherwise called Willim Thomas Willims to be my lawfull true and sole Exequitor to order and dispose of my goodes and so requeste this my laste will and testamente in all pointes and [...] thereof as I repose in him my sevriall confidence to whom after my debtes paid my severall expenses discharged and all and singular my legacies performed, I give and bequeathe the reste and [...] of all and singular my goods chattells and creditts whatsoever.

Item I doe by this my laste will and testamente utterlie revoke [...] annull and make [...] all and everie other former testamentes voidded, legacies bequestes, Exequetors and overseers by me [...] before this time made voidded or bequeathed.

Item I doe appointe and ordaine my righte trustie and wellbeloved friende Sir Roland Stanley of Hooton, Knighte & Henrie Moston of Cawe [?] Edward Willims and Edward Theloalle Esquires to be overseers of this my laste will and testamente.

Item all further debtes as are owinge unto me abrode in other handes are written in a schedule to this my will annexed subscribed with my owne hand [...] forthe as my memorie serves at the makinge hereof. In notice whereof I have caused this my laste will and testamente to be written and to the same hand putt my seale and subscribed my name the date and yeare above mentioned in the partie [?] of the witnesses undernamed Beinge Thomas Win ap Willim. Henrie Moston. Robert Harrie clerke, John Martin clerke Thomas Ffletcher notarie publique Griffith Ffletcher notarie publique.

3. Last Will & Testamente of Sir William Williams of Vaynol, 1625

In the name of God Amen, The seaventh daie of May in the yeare of our Lord God One thousand six hundred twenty and five, and in the sixth yeare of the reigne of our Soveraigne Lord Charles by the grace of God of England, Scotland, Ffrance and Ireland Kinge, defender of the faithe. I Sir William Williams of Vaynol in the Countie of Carnarvon Baronnett beinge sicke in bodie but of sound and perfect memorie praise bee to God, doe make and ardaine this my last will and testament in writinge in manner and forme following that is to saie, ffirst I commend my soule to Amightie God my maker hopeing assuredly to bee saved by the blessed [...] death and passion of Jesus Christ my blessed saviour and redeemer. And I commend my bodie to the tombe within the Cathedrall Church of Bangor wherein my late ffather was interred.

Item I bequeath towards the reparacon of the said Cathedrall Church of Bangor six shillings and eight pence.

Item I bequeath towards the reparacon of the parish Church of Llanddeiniolen five shillings. Another five shillings towards the reparacon of the Church of Llandegay.

Item I bequeath to the poor people of the parish of Bangor twenty shillings to bee equallie divided between them and twenty shillings more to the poor people of the parish of Llandeiniolen to bee equallie divided between them.

Item whereas I have heretofore assigned certain messuages, lands and Tente. [tenements] with appurtennce in the Townes, fields, Hamletts burroughs and precincts of Bangor, Maynol Bangor, Pentir and Carnarvon and in the ffranchises and liberties of the said Town or Burough of Caernvon [sic] within the said Countie of Carnarvon to retaine y [...] of the intent and purpose to raise the Some of foure hundred pounds apiece marriage porcon to Margaret Williams and Elnor Williams to of the younger daughters of the said Sir William Williams.

Now in regard of the naturall love and affecon which I have and beare towards my said two younger daughters Margarett and Elnor, and for their greater preferment [in marriage] I give devise and bequeath to my said daughter Margaret Williams in further augmentation of her marriage porcon the some of two hundred threescore and six poundes thirteen shillings and fower pence to bee paid her in forme following viz, a hundred pounds thereof that daie twelve month next ensuinge the daie of my decease, and the some of one hundred pounds that daie two years next after my decease, and the some of threescore six pounds thirteen shillings foure pence being the residue of the said two hundred threescore and six poundes thirteen shillings and fower pence soe hereby bequeathed unto her the said magarett in augmentation of her marriage porcon as aforesaid maie bee fully paid her within three yeares next after my decease.

Item I give devise and bequeath unto my said daughter Elnor Williams in further augmentation of her marriage porcon the some of two hundred pounds to be likewise paid her in forme followinge viz a hundred poundes thereof that daie twelve months next ensuinge the date of my decease, and the like some of one hundred pounds that daie two yeares next after my decease Whereby all the said two hundred pounds soe hereby bequeathed unto her the said Elenor in augmentacon of her marriage porcon as aforesaid maie bee fullie paid her within two yeares next after my decease.

Item I give devise and bequeath unto my younger Sonne Henry Williams all & singular those messuaged lands, tents and hereditaments with Thappurtenncs within the hundred of Yssaph [in the Castell township in the Conwy Valley] in the Countie of Caernvon [sic] which I have formerly conveyed and assured to and to this of the said Henry Williams and his heires, and all the other messuages lande tents and hereditamentes whatsoever with thappurtenncs which I have or ought to have in Y Ssaph aforsaid. To have and to hold all the said premises to the aforesaid Henry Williams my Sonne and to the heires males of his bodie lawfullie begotten. The remainder thereof in default of such issue to bee and remaine to my right heires forever.

Item I give devise and bequeath to the said Henry Williams my younger sonne eight oxen with the plough and plough irons and other incidents belonginge thereunto.

Also twent four milch kyne with their calves and a bull to follow them. Alsoe twelve beastes of three and four yeares old, a mare and two fillies, a Coult of three yeares old and threescore sheep.

Item I give devise and bequeath to my said sonne Henry Williams two featherbeds, two coverlets, a goblet of silver, six silver spoones with a brasen mortar and pestle, one bedsteed.

Item I give devise and bequeath to the said Henry Williams the Some of one hundred pounds of current money of England.

Item I doe make ordaine constitute and appoint my eldest Sonne and heire Thomas Williams to bee my lawfull true and sole Executre of this my last will and testament to order and dispose my goods and to execute this my last will and testament in all pointes & articles thereof as I repose in him my Beriall confidence to whom after my debts paid, my funeral expenses discharged and all and singular my goods Cattells Chattells and Creditts whatsoever.

And as for my eldeste daughter Elizabeth Williams and her marriage porcon, her eldeste brother the said Thomas Williams hath allreadie given her Securitie for the same. And I doe hereby referre her for further augmentation of her marriage porcon, to her said brother Thomas Williams as he shall think convenient whom I hope will (out of his natural love and affection towardes her) treat her kindly and loveningly.

Item I doe by this my last will and testament utterly revoke, [...] annul and make [...] all of the everie other former Testament and wills before by mee made. In witness whereof I have caused this my last will and testament to bee written, and to the same have putt my Seale and subscribed m name the daie and yeare above mentioned in the pr'ce of Wil. Williams of Vaynoll, read, signed, seales, published and acknowledged in the pr'ce of Edm. Griff., John Wynn, William Owen de Brondeg, Katherin Williams, Robert Bunde, John Gruffith, Richard Boulton.

4. The Anwyl Manuscript, Brogyntyn MSS
Written by Lewis Anwyl of Park[83]

1634. I was married the second tyme the 6th daye of ffebruarye being ffrydae att Vaynol in Carnarvonshire with Magdalen the only Daughter of Sir Thomas Wilhams Baronett. I beinge then of about the age of 38 yeares, and she of 23 or thereabouts. My father and ffather in lawe being then present.

My ffather in lawe Sir Thomas Wilhims Dyed at Vaynol uppon a sundaye morning about 5 of the cloke the 26 Daye of June 1636 beinge then about the age of 50 yeares, his sonne and heyre Sir Wilham Wilhams being then in France he was buried privately in the night att Bangor, without either funeral sermon or after, or other commemoracion, he was the sonne of Sir Wilham Wilhams the sonne of Thomas Wynne ap Wilham, a youner sonne of the house Cychwyllan.

My ffather was Sheriffe of Carnarvonshire the year 1634 but beganne his office before the allhollantide the year before.

I left Vaynol and together with my wife Magdalen came to live at Kemmes the ffirst of August 1634, the next Christmas after, we were ffaigne to go to Chester, to the ladye Wilhams to live with her: my wife remayned there untill after the next Whitsontide, being sickelye, and then came backe againe to Kemes.

My mother in lawe the ladye Catherine Wilhamses dyed at Priscol in Carnarvonshire upon Thursdaye the 14th daye of November 1639, between 9 and 10 of the clocke att night and was buried in Bangor Church upon the Sundaye night followinge without sermon or other commemoration, she was the eldest daughter of Robert Wynne of Conweye, a younger brother of the house of Gwydder, her mother was Dorothye Dymocke of Willington in Fflintshire. She was about 51 or 52 yeares of age when she dyed, her sonne Sir Wilham Wilhams was then highe Sheriffe of Carnarvonshire.

5. Last Will & Testamente of Sir William Williams of Vaynol, 1658

I Sir William Williams of Vaynol in the Countie of Carnarvon Baronnett beinge weake in bodie but of good and perfecte memorie praise bee to God, and calling to remembrance the certaintie of Fate of this transitente life doe make and ordaine this my last will and testament in manner and forme following revoking and annulling by there presents all and every testamente and testaments, will and willes heretofore by mee made ande ordained eythir by words or writinge, and this to bee taken only for my last will and testament and noe other. And first and principally I commend my soule to Almighty God my creator Assuredly believing that I shall receive full pardon and full remission of all my Sinnes & bee saved by the death and passions of my blessed Saviour & Redeemer Chris Jesus. And my bodie to be layed in my owne vault in the late Cathedral Church of Bangor. And my burial in a [ ] manner [ ] to my Quallities. And as for and touching whatt temporall state the Lord hath bin pleased to bestowe upon mee and for the settlings thereof whereby noe strife or confrontation may happen amongst my surviving friends about the same after my decease my will and mianinge is that the same shallbe ymployed Disposed and setled in a manner and forme hereafter appraised.

And first I give and bequeath towards the reparation of the parishe Churche of llandeiniolen tenne shillings. Towards to reparation of the parishe church of Llanberis tenne shillings. Towards the reparation of the parishe church of Llandair tenne shillings. Towards the reparation of the parishe church of Llanengel tenne shillings. Towards the reparation of the parishe church of Llanbeblicke tenne shillings.

And as it hath not pleased god to bestowe me with any issue by my now wife and in regard of her greate love and affection towards mee as alsoe her paynes in ordering my house and familie I give devise and bequeath unto my said loveing wife All these my messuages lands and tenements, houses shoppes barnes stables gardens, orchads, banksides situate, lyeing and being the parish of Llanbeblike and within the towne and liberties of Carnarvon formerly settled upon her issue by my deed in writinge bearinge the date twoe and twentieth daye of Ffebruarie in the yeare of our Lorde one Thousand Six Hundred Ffiftie and two unto which for more certaintie I [ ] myself unto.

And likewise I give devise and bequeath unto my said loving wife all that my Messuage and tenements of land in Castell-maye comonly called or known by the name of Spitt ... Gwynt and that Share of Tythynn Llwydyn which I have lately purchased of Haubert Roland gent. To have and to holde the aforsaid which I promised for and duringe the term of her naturall life.

Item I give and bequeathe to my servant William Evans Twenty pounds yearly during his life.

Item I give and bequeathe to my servant William Williams Six ounds yearly during his life.

Item I give and bequeathe to my servant Rytheuch Jones fortie shillings yearly during his life.

Item I give and bequeath to my servant Gabriell Hughes five pounds yearly during his life.

Item I give and bequeath to my servante Ellis Price three pounds yearly during his life.

Item I give and bequeath to my servant Owen Johnson fower poundes yearly during his life.

Item I give and bequeath to my servant Richard Davies five pounds yearly during his life.

Item I give and bequeath to my servant William Price fortie shilline yearly during his life.

And my will and meaninge is that the severall Annuities before named shall be yearly satisfied and payed out of Messuaged lands and Tenements hereafter verified.

My will is that the twenty pounds yearly by me bequeathed to my servant William Evans that hee my said servant shall yearly receive all the rents issues and proffitts of that my Tenement called [ ] in the Comatt of Tallibolion in the Countie of Anglesey duringe the terme of his natierall life according to my aforesaid bequest.

And my will and meaninge is that the rest of the said Annuities by me herein bequeathed shall be yearly paid unto my afornamed Servants out of the issue and proffitts of the severall Messuage lands and Tenements hereafter mentioned. That is to say in Tythyn [ ] now in the tenure of Rowland Owne & Griffith ap Ellis. Tythyn y Cum glas late in the tenure of Alice Griffith deceased and now in the tenure of Williams Lloyd and sevrall more premises are situated lueinge and beinge in the parish of Llanberis. And also my Tenement in Rythallt now in the tenure of William Williams. And also that Tenement in Rythallt aforesaid in the tenure of Morris ap William ap Evan. And my will and meaninge is that my heyre shall yearly paye unto my aforesaid servants the severall Annuities and of the proffitts of the premises at the Ffeaste of All Saints yearly duringe their severall natural lives.

Item I give John [ ] my Sonnes tutor fortie pounds. And my will is that duringthe tyme hee shall continue with my said Sonne hee shall have twenty ounds yearly it being his new stipend or wage, both which Somes my will is shall be payed out of the rents issue and proffitts of these lands that now disend unto my said Sonne and not formerly estate.

Item I give and bequeath to Richard Willams my [ ] servant tenne pounds to be likewise raised out of the aforesaid lands which shall now disend unto my saide Sonne and not formerly estates as aforesaid.

Item I give and bequeath unto my servant Symon Cedyill five pounds. To my servant John Crane five poundes. Item I give and bequeath to my servant Griffith ap John Girffith ffortie shillings. Item I give and beqeath to Gwen five pounds to be paid her within Halfe a year after my decease if shee bee then living.

Item I give devise and bequeath one moiety of all and smauler my goods chattills and credits and by mee herein not given or bequeathd my debts legalised and funeral expenses first paid and discharged unto my loveinge wife Dame Margaret Williames. And another moyetie of the premises unto my deare Sonne Griffith Williames Esquire. And I doe hereby ordaine constitute and appointe my aforesaid loving wife Dame Margaret Williams and my deare Sonne Griffith Williames Esquire to bee executors of this my last will and testament.

Item I doe nominate and appointe my deare [ ] Henry Williams esquire, my Deare Brother Thomas Williams Esquire, my loveinge Cousens Thomas Madrin and Robert Wynne Esquires and my loveing father in law Griffith Jones Esquire to be overseers of this my last will & Testament & [ ] Desire them to affoard their best advise and assistance to my said executors in the execution of this my last will. : William Williams, Stated, Published and declared to bee my last will and testament Tho: Madrin, John Wynne, Henry Williames, Thomas Williames, Robert Wynne, Oen Wynne, William Arthur, Willam Williames.

7. Marriage Settlement of Margaret Jones and Sir William Williams of Vaynol, 14 April 1640[84]

This indenture made the 18th daie of March in the 15th year of the raigne of our Sovraigne Lord Charles by the grace of God of England, Scotland, France and Ireland Kinge defender of the faith, between Gruffith Jones of Castellmarch in the Countie of Carnarvon Esquire of the one parte and Jane Jones second daughter of the said Gruffith Jones begotten by the Bodie of Marie his now wife on the other parte. Whereas William Gruffith late of Carnarvon in the Countie of Carnarvon esquire the said Gruffith Jones and Marie his wife for and in [...] and [...] of [...] of agreement bearinge date the thirteenth daie of Julie in the twentieth yeare of the raigne of our late sovraign Lord James of famous memorie over England and over Scotland, the eiyth and [...] made be forever the said William Gruffith of the one parte and William Jones of Castellmarch in the said County Esquier of the other parte att the conclusion of a marriage thereafter to be [...] and solemnized between the said Gruffith Jones and Marie his wife wich afterwarde tooke effect heretofor att his Majestie's Great Sessions held at Caernarfon in the said countie of Caernarfon upon mondaie, being the Twentieth Daie of August in the fourteenth year of his said Majestie's raigne that now is, before [...] and Robert B [...] wood Esquires, his Majestie's Justices of the said Great Sessions, same acknowledged and leavied one fine for cognizance de droit come [...] de [Lonn?] done [London?] with proclamacions thereupon unto Thomas Glyn of Glynllivon in the Countie of Carnarvon afore said Esquire and John Glyn of Lincolns Inn in the Countie of Midd[lesex] Esquire, of all that capital messuage of the said William Gruffith and the gardens, backe-[...], Orchards, Lands, meadows and pasture thereunto belonging or therewith used and occupied, and of all those houses, barnes, stables, gardens and tenemente [...] or late before in the sevrall tenures of [...] Morris Robert ap Howell and William Gruffith being in Carnarvon aforesaid and the liberties thereof and of all those Messuages, tenements and lands called Llanvair, Drws [?] y Coed, [...] y ddwy Afon [...] Mawryny [...] and [...] Rûg [...] and being in the township of Llanvair Isgaer, [...] Dinlley [...] and Kay in the said Countie of Carnarvon and of all other the messuages, lande, tenements and hereditaments of the said William Gruffith being in the said Countie of Carnarvon whereof he or anie other to his said [...] seised of anie estate of inheritance the thirtieth Daie of Julie in the [...] yeare of the raigne of our said late soveraigne Lord Kinge James and also the messuages, land, tenements and hereditaments of John Gruffith Esquier deceased father of the said William Gruffith [...] or anie other to his [...] was seizesd of his estate of inheritance att the time of his death comprised in the said fine by the name or names of one hundred messuages, ffourtie tofte, one hundred gardens, two thousand acres of land, a thousand acres of meadow, two thousand acres of pasture, sixtie acres of woode, two hundred acres of [...] and barns, a hundred acres of [...] and two hundred acres of turbarie with the appurtenances in Carnarvon. Llanfair Isgaer, Pennarth [?] Pennant [?] Rug, Dynlle and [...] and whereas by an Indenture bearinge date the twentieth Daie of August in the fowerteenth yeare of the reigne of his said Majestie that nowe is, the said fine was declared to be to severall uses in the said indenture expressed. In with said Indenture there is one provision contained in these woorde, or to the like effect following, provided below that if maie and shall be Lawefull to and for the said William Gruffith and Sir William Jones during these [...] times, and to and for the said William Gruffith and Gruffith Jones during these [...] times after the decease of the said Sir

William Jones Knight, by these [...] deale in writing under these hands and seales att said time and terms and from tyme to tyme to aulter [...] or make voide all or anie the uses or estates afore said touchinge the sevverall promiss afore said, or anie part or parcell thereof, and by the same deale, or anie other [...] deale under these hands and seales testified by fower relible witnesses, to limmit and appoint anie newe use or uses hereof and that the said fine and fines shall be and eaver, and the said Thomas Glyn and John Glyn and ther servs [?] [...] stand and be seized [...] of the premissess [...] the use or uses [...] be aultered, changed [...] or made voide and aforesaid to such newe uses and limitacons, limites and [...] as afresaid. Anything in these presente to [?] the [?] contrarie thereof in anie wise not withstanding and by the said indenture [...] anne wise was there is a marraidge had and solemnized between Sir William Williams and Margaret Jones, eldeste daughter of the said Gruffith Jones and Marie his wife. and whereas the said Sir William Jones and William Gruffith in consideracion of the said maraidge, and for and towards [...] of the marraidge porcion of the said Margaret Jones resolved to repeale, revoke [...] and make voide all and everie the use and uses estate and estates in the said [...] indenture, lymited, expressed and declared, and to limitt and declare newe uses and estates thereof and therby to setle the said lands and all and singular said premises [...] upon Dame Margaret and Sir William Williams and their children and other persons in such maner as by an indenture tripartate [?] made the fowerteenth daie of Aprill in the Presente yeere of the raigne of our said Sovraigne Lord Charles between the said Sir William Jones, by the name of Sir William Jones, Knight, one of his Majestie's Justices at his [...] Bench at Westminster, and the said William Gruffith of the first parte and the said Gruffith Jones, by the name of Gruffith Jones of Castellmarch in the Countie of Carnarvon Esquire, son and heire apparent of the said Sir William Jones, of the second parte, and the said Sir William Williams, by the name of Sir William Williams of Vainol in the said Countie of Carnarvon Barronett, of the third part, the sume [?] is att large [...] whereby the said Sir William Jones and William Gruffith according to the power and authoritie given unto them by the provisoe aforesaid and in perchance [?] thereof for the consideracions aforesaid and by the said last [...] deale signed with these hands and sealed with these seales in the presence of fower realible wittnessess att the leaste declared for and concerninge the messuages, land, tenements and hereditaments and premises whereof any use or estate is in and by the said first rental [?] indenture limited, expressed [?] and declared that the said fine [...] be and ever, and that the cognizances therein named and there [signed and sealed?] be and stand seized thereof and of every part and parcell thereof to the uses intentes and purposes and [...] to the liberties, powers and provisoes in the said last [...] deale expressed [...] and declared and to and for noe other uses [...] or purposes whatsoever, wherein there is a provisoe that it shall and mai be lawefull and for the said Gruffith Jones att anie time or tymes for and duringe the tyme, terme and – of seaven yeares next after the decease of the said William Gruffith, if the said Gruffith Jones happen to survive the said William Gruffith, to – for one and twentie yeares in possession those two tenements called and known by the names of Talmignith [?] and the lands of the said William Griffith in Llanvair Isgaer [...] the said premisess on and of them or any part, parcell or member thereof to the use and towards the advancement and performance of the said Jane Jones Second daughter of the said Gruffith Jones att the yearly rents following [...] Talmigneth, att the yearly rent of two shillinge or more and the said lande in Llanvair Isgaer att the yearly rents of two shillinge or more, and by the said sevrall indentures nowe at large [...]. Nowe this [...] indenture wittness by [...] the said Gruffith Jones for the advancement and performancs of the said Jane Jones and in [...] of the said provisoe and power [...] him as aforesaid by the said [...] indentures according to the fine meaneinge thereto late demised, granted and to ffarme, lett [?] and sett [?] and by [...] said rents doth demise, grante and to ffarme, lett and sett [?] unto the said Jane Jones the said [...] tenemente called and known by the names of Talmigneth and the lande of William Gruffith in Llanvair Isgaer part and parcells of the said premisses of the severall and [...] appurtenances. To lande and etc and [...] all and singular the said two tenemente with there to sevrall and [...] appurtenances unto the said Jane Jones her [...] and assignes from the makening thereof for and duringe the full(?) one(?) and terms of one and twenty years in possession next after to come and immediately to [...] the Daie and the date of these present att and under the yearly rents followinge [...] Talmigneth att the rent of two shillinge and six(?) pence and the said lande in Llanvair att the rent of two shillinge and six pence to be yearly paid to the said Gruffith Jones oweinge/owneinge for long a tyme of the said tearme as he shall happen to live and paying -- ------- likewise after his decesse(?) ----- --- said ------ the said rente of two shillinge six pence for Talmigneth and thesaid rente of two shillinge six pence for the said lande in Llanvair Isgaer dureinge such and for long a time of the said tearme as he shall happen to live. after the decease of the said Gruffith Jones and Marie to such person or persons as the imediat remainder, indenture and [...] of the said [...] by and after the decease of the said Gruffith Jones and Marie shall remayne and come befor(?) of the said [...] provided allwaies that if the said Gruffith Jones shall or will att anie time hereafter [...] the compasse of seaven yeares next after the deceasse of the said William Gruffith paie or or raise to be paid or [...] to or to the use of the said Jane Jones her executors administrators or assigns the summe of ffive shillinge of current money of England att or within the [...] chapill or towne Halle of Carnarvon or att the front door thereof if the summe be [...] that then and from thenceforth this present deed and the grant thereby made of the [...] and every thing therein contained shall utterly cease, determine and be utterlie voyd and of noe effect to all intente and purpose. Annie thing in these presenth contained to the contrarie thereof anie wise not withstandinge. In witness hereof both parties to these present Interchangeably ane part these hands and seales the day and yeare first above written. 1640.

8. Marriage Settlement of Griffith and Penelope Williams, 25 July 1666[85]

This indenture made the five and twentieth day of July in the seaventeenth year of the raigbe of our soveraigne Lord Charles the Second by the grace of God of England, Scotland, Ffrance and Ireland Kinge, Defender of the

Ffaith.

Betweene Sir Griffith Williams of Vaynol in the County of Caernarfon Barronet of the one Partie [and] Robert Lord Bulkeley Viscount Cafsilis in Ireland of Baron Hill in the County of Anglesey, Thomas Bulkeley of Dynas in the said County of Caernarfon Esq., Sir Roger Mostyn of Mostyn in the County of Fflint Knight and Barronett, Piers Lloyd the younger of Ligwy in the said County of Anglesey Esq., and Richard Wynne of Branas in the County of Merioneth Esq., of the other partie.

Witnesseth that for the Cuttinge of and debarring of all entails and right of [...] of in and unto All and Singular the messuages, Lands, tenements, rents and hereditaments herein after mentioned and that as will for and in Consideration of a marriage heretofore had and solmenised between him the said Sir Griffith Williams and Dame Penelope his now wife as alsoe of a considerable marriage portion by him the said Sir Griffith had and [...] with the said Dame Penelope and for the settlinge, conveyinge and assuringe of the said messuages, lands, tenements and hereditaments with thappurtenances [...] afor mentioned accordinge as herein after is expressed and for the well limittinge of a jointure upon the said Dame Penelope in [...] of her Dower out of all the messuages, Lands, tenements and hereditaments of the said Sir Griffith Williams and for diverse other good and lawfull considerations him hereunto [...]. It is covenanted and agreed by and betweene the said parties that the said Sir Griffith Williams shall and will att or before the next greate Sessions after the daye hereof to be holden and kept [?] in and for the said county of Caernarfon in due forme of law acknowledge and leavy [?] unto the said Robert Lord Bulkeley and Thomas Bulkeley and the heirs of the said Robert Lord Bulkeley one ffine sir cognizance de droit come ceog [?] ouf/out de London to be ingrossed and recorded with proclamations thereupon accordinge to the forms of the statute in that case made and provided of and upon All that his Capitall Messuage and all the Demeasne lands and appurtenances thereunto belonginge, commonly called and known by the name of Vaynol situate lyinge and beinge in the sevrall parishes of Bangor, Pentir and Llanddeiniolen in the said County of Caernarfon and of and upon all other the messuages, Lands, tenements, rents and hereditaments whatsoever with thappurtennes where he the said Sir Griffith Williams hath or ought to have in possession, Revertion, Remainder, trust or use within the said County of Caernarfon and where heretofore were the messuages, Lands, tenements, rents and hereditaments of Sir William Williams Bartt the late deceased father of the said Sir Griffith Williams and of and upon the Revertion and Revertions, Rents and Services thereof and every part and parcell thereof All to be comprized in the said ffine by the name or names of fowre hundred messuages, two hundred tofts, seaven milnes, two pigeon houses, five hundred gardens, seven thousand acres of Land, six thousnad acres of meadow, six thousand acres of pasture, five hunded acres of wood, three thousand acres of heath and brury and two hundred acres of moor and also tenne pound writ, three severall piscaries and three wears with th'appurtenances in Bangor, Maynol Bangor, Carredog, Treborth, Tregroyrrhyddion, Pentir, Dinorwick, als Dinorwig, Llanrûg, Rûg, Llanfair Isgaer, Bottandreg, Castellmay, Carnarvon, Llanbeblicke, Rhuddallt, Treflan, Bettus Garmon, Dolbadarn, Llan Erw, Llandeiniolen, Llanlyfni and Tre'rrSaint or by such other name or names, quantities and description of [...] as to the said parties shall sceme [?] with.

And of the said ffine soe, or to the effect aforesaid, had and leavied, and all and every other fine and fines leavied or to be leavied between the said parties of the premises or any part thereof shall be and [...] and the said Robert Lord Bulkeley and Thomas Bulkeley Cognizers therein named and their heirs shall by vertue thereof be and stand seized of all and singular the premises with their, and every of their, appurtenances to the severall uses and behoofes intents and purposes herein after [...] expressed and declared touching and [...]. All and Singular the said Capitall Messuage and all the Demeasne Lands and appurtenances thereunto belonginge comonly called and known by the name of Vaynol lyinge and beinge in the severall parishes of Bangor, Pentir and Llandeiniolen aforesaid.
[*The next long section details each and every parcel of land in Llandeiniolen and the current tenant*]
[...] and allother the messauges, lands, tenements, rents and hereditaments whatsoever with th'appurtenances of him the said Sir Griffith Williams, situate, lyinge and beinge in Pentir and Bangor

aforesaid. (Except one parcell of land, meadow and pasture called Cae'r Sherrie and one yard land in Tyllvayre canol in the township of Tregwyrrhyddion and parish of Bangor aforesaid heretofore conveyed by the said Sir William Williams to Owen Parry of Perfeddgoed in the said County of Caernarfon gent and now in possession in exchange for severall parcells of lands of his the said Owen Parrys in Tregwyrrhyddion aforesaid conveyed to the said Sir William Williams and in these [...] and the said fine to be continued.) beinge part and parcell of the premises in the said ffine comprized the said ffine shall be and [...] and said Robert Lord Bulkeley and Thomas Bulkeley Cognizes therein named and their heirs shall stand and be thereof seized to the use and behoofe of the said Sir Griffith Williams and Dame Penelope his wife for and duringe the terme of their naturall lives and the life of the longer liver of them without impeachment of waste duringe the life of the said Sir Griffith Williams for and in the name of the Jointure of the said Dame Penelope and in lieu and barre of the dower that may to her [...] out of one of the messuages, lands, tenements, rents and hereditaments of the said Sir Griffith Williams.

And as touching and concerninge the said parcell called Cae'r Sherrie and the yard land in Talvayre canol aforesaid the said ffine shall be and enure touching the rest and residue of the premises comprized in the said ffine, whereof noe estate is herein before limmited the said ffine shall be and enure and the said Robert Lord Bulkeley and Thomas Bulkeley cognizers therein named and their heirs shall stand and be thereof seized to the use and behoofe of the said Owen Parry his heirs and assifns for ever. And as all and singular the premises whereof noe estate of inheritance is herein before limitted from and after the end and determination of the estates for [...] aforesaid and as the same shall [...] end and determine the said ffine shall be and enure and the said Robert Lord Bulkeley and Thomas Bulkeley cognizers therein named and their heirs shall stand and be thereof seized to the use and behoofe of the said Robert Lord Bulkeley, Thomas Bulkeley, Sir Roger Mostyn, Piers Lloyd and Richard Wynne for and duringe the naturall life of the said Sir Griffith Williams in trust and to the intent to preserve the contingent estates thereof herein after limitted from beinge destroyed or avoyded and to doe every such act or acts as is, are or shall be requisite for that purpose by entry or otherwise. And from and after the end and determination of all the estates aforesaid and as the same shall [...] end and determine to the use and behoofe of the first son of the body of the said Sir Griffith Williams on the bdy of the said Dame Penelope to be begotten and of the heirs males of the body of such first son lawfully issuing and in default of such issue then to the use and behoofe of the second son of the body of the said Sir Griffith Williams on the bdy of the said Dame Penelope to be begotten and of the heirs males of the body of such second son lawfully issuing [...] [*This then continues up to the sixth son*]

And in default of such issue then to the use and behoofe of every other son and sons of the body of the body of the said Sir Griffith Williams on the bdy of the said Dame Penelope to be begotten and of the heirs males of the body of such first son lawfully issuing of the said Sir Griffith William on the body of the said Dame Penelope to be begotten and of the heirs males of the body of every such other son and sons lawfully issuing successively one after another and by way of remainders intaile to every such other son and sons and the heirs males of his body as they and every of them shall happen to be in seniority and priority of birth the elder of every such other sayd son and sons and the heirs of his body begotten to be still preferred and to take place before the younger and ther heirs of his body begotten.

And in default of such issue then to the use and behoofe of the first daughter of the body of the said Sir Griffith Williams on the body of the said Dame Penelope to be begotten and of the heirs of the body of such first daughter lawfully issuing. And in default of such issue then to the use and behoofe of the second daughter [etc., etc. down to the sixth daughter] And in default of such issue then to the use and behoofe of every other daughter and daughters of the body of the said Sir Griffith Williams on the body of the said Dame Penelope to be begotten and of the heirs of the body of every such other daughter and daughters lawfully issuing successively one after another and by way of remainders in taile to every such other daughter and daughters as they and every of them shall happen to be in seniority and priority of birth, the elder of every such other daughter and daughters an the heirs of her body begotten to be still preferred and to be place before the younger and the heirs of her body begotten in such manner and sort as is herein before limitted to the first six daughters and not jointly or together.

And in default of such issue then to the use and behoofe of the heirs of the body of the said Sir Girffith Williams on the body of the said Dame Penelope to be begotten. And in default of such issue then to such use and behoofes intents and purposes as the said Sir Griffith Williams shall be in deed or will in writing to be by him [...] sealed executed and publyshed in the presence of these or more relible witnesses, disect, limitt and appoint and to and for noe other use intent or purpose whatsoever provided always and it is covenanted, granted and agreed by and between the said parties to these present and it is the [...] remaininge of these present and of the parties to the forme that it shall and may be lawfull to and for the said Sir Griffith Williams att any time or times hereafter att his own will and pleasure for any causes and considerations to him foorminge good by his deed in writing, sealed and delivered in the presence of three or more credible witnesses to limmit appoint or declare any use or uses of all those messuages, lands, tenements and hereditamentswich situate and beinge in the severall parishes of Llanberis, Llanvair isgaer, Llanrûg, Llanbeblick and Llanllyfni in the said County of Caernarfon to and for such person or persons his and their Executors, Administrators and assigns for and during the full term and space of ninetie nine years to comence in possession, revertion, remainder or otherwise and att such time and upon such contingencies as he shall limmitt or appoint and from and after such limitation appointment or declaration then the [...] to these presents and their heirs shall be and stand thereof seized to such uses and purposes as shall be therein declared for and duringe the said terme and the said ffine and all other fines and other assureances had leavied or made or to be hereafter had leavied or made of the premises shall be and enure to the uses and purposes as shall be therein declared for and duringe the said terme all and every the uses and estates in these [...] inconseqent therewith [...] or givinge way thereunto duringe the continuance thereof and after the said terme determined to such other uses and behoofes as are herein before limitted for and [...] the same Anythinge herein before confirmed to the contrary thereof many wise notwithstanding In Witness whereof the said Griffith Williams hath to these present interchangeabbly sett his hand and seale the day and year in these presents first written Anno Dni: 1665.

Grf Williams

5. Last Will & Testamente of Sir William Williams of Vaynol, 1695

In the Name of God Amen I Sir William Williams of Vaenol in the County of Caernarvon Barrt do make publish and declare this my last will and Testament in manner and form following.

Whereas by an Indenture bearing Date on or abt the 24 day of June in the year of our Lord 1695 I have given and granted unto Ch: Allanson and his Heir one annuity or yearly Rent Charge of £540 using and going out of all my Mannors Land and Tenements & Hereditaments whatsoever to hold the said Annuity or Rent Charge unto the said C: Allanson his Heirs and Assigns from and after my Decease and failure of Sons of my Body. Now I do hereby ratify and confirm the said Grant, and my Will and meaning is that the said C.A. his Heirs and Assigns shall and may have hold receive and take the said Annuity or Yearly Change according to the purpose, true intent and meaning of the said Indenture and I do hereby Will and Devise the said C.A. to take care and look after the Due Execution of my hereafter Bequests and Devises and as concerning all my real Estates and Estates whatsoever subject and liable to the said Annual and Years Rent Charge of £540 and subject and liable to such Incumbrances or Securities as I have heretofore made and or shall hereafter make for the Securing of any sum or sums of money forth out of or by said Real Estate or any part or parcel thereof I give and devise and bequeath the same as is herein after mentioned (that is to say my will and mind) and I do hereby Give Devise and Bequeath all and every my mannors, Lordships, Capital Messuage, Land, Tenements, Tythes, and Hereditaments with their and every of the rights members and appurtenances Situate lying and being within the several Counties of Caernarvon and Anglesey or within any other place or County whatsoever within the Kingdom of England or Dominion of Wales or elsewhere in case I do depart this life without Heirs of my Body lawfully begotten and not otherwise until, and for the life of Sir Bourchier Wrey of Tawstock in the County of Devon Bart for and During the Term of his natural life without impeachment of or for any manner of want and from and after the decease of the said B.W. I do give devise and Bequeath the same unto and to the use of B.W. son of the said B.W. for and during the term of his natural life without impeachment or for any manner of want and from and after the decease of the said BW I do give devise and Bequeath the same unto and to the use of Chichester Wrey son of the said Sir BW for and during the term of his natural life without impeachment of or for any manner of want and from and after the decease of the said Chichester Wrey then unto and to the Use of our Sovereign Lord King William his assigns and Successors for ever subject and liable nevertheless to the Rent Charge and Incumbrances as afore concerning the personal estate which I shall leave at the time of my Decease of whatsoever the same shall consist. I do hereby give Devise and bequeath the same unto the said C.A. of the Middle Temple Esq and John Evans of Bangor in the County of Caernarfon Gent my present Steward whom I hereby make full and sole Executors of this my last will and testament and not Executors in trust but to the interest that they may have the same for their own uses by Legacies and Debts upon simple Contract and, funeral expenses being first deducted and paid thereout, I do give and bequeath unto every menial Servant which shall be with me at the time of my Decease £5 apiece to buy them mourning withal, and I do hereby revoke and make void all former Wills and Testaments by me at any time heretofore made in writing or otherwise, In Wittness whereof I the said Sir William Williams have hereunto set my hand and Seal the 25th day of June in the year of our Lord 1695.

Signed sealed and published by the said Sir WW in our presence and by us attested in his presence the day and year above written

    Henry Maisterman   Mott Richards   Jnr Commons

9. Granting of the Faenol estate by King William III to John Gore, 1699[83]

William the Third by the Grace of God of England Scotland France and Ireland King, Defender of the Faith and Etc. To all to whom, these present Letters shall come, Greeting.

Whereas our beloved and faithful Subject Sir William Williams late of Vaynol in the County of Caernarfon, Bart. Now deceased in his Lifetime to wit on the 23rd Day of June in the year of our Lord 1695 in due Form of Law made his last Will and Testament in writing and in the same Will reciting that he, the said Sir Wm Williams by a certain [...] Bearing Date on or about the 24th day of June in the year of our Lord 1695 have given and granted to one Charles Allanson and his Heirs on Annuity or yearly Rent Charge of £540 to be issuing out of all his Manors Landes Tenements and Hereditaments wheresoever to hold the said annuity of yearly Rent Charge unto the said Charles Allanson his heirs and Assigns immediately after the Death of the said Sir Wm Williams by his same Will ratified and confirmed the said Grant to the said Chas. Allanson and his Heirs so as aforesaid made.

And as to the real Estate and Estates whatsoever of the said Sir Wm Williams subject to the said Annuity of £540 and such other Incumbrances and Securities by the said Sir Wm Williams the made or to be made for Security of any money from or out of the said real Estate or any part of parcel thereof He the said Sir Wm Williams gave devised and bequeathed in manner and form following, to wit, he devised and bequeathed all and singular his Manors Lordships capital Messuage Lands Rents Reversions Mills Tythes Tenements and Hereditaments with their rights Members and Appurtenances whatsoever situate lying and being in the said Counties of Carnarvon and Anglesey or in any other place of County whatsoever within the Kingdom of England and Anglesey or in any other place or County whatsoever within the Kingdom of England and Dominion of Wales or elsewhere (if the said Sir Williams should depart this Life without heirs of his body lawfully begotten and not otherwise) to Sir Bourchier Wrey then of Tawstock in the County of Devon Bart. (Now deceased) and, to the use of the said Bourchier Wrey for and during the Terms of his natural Life without Impeachment of Waste and after his Death the aforesaid sir Wm Williams by his same Will gave, devised and bequeathed the said premises to Bourchier Wrey (now Sir Bourchier Wrey Bart.) son of the before named Bourchier Wrey and to the use of the said Bourchier Wrey the son then the said Sir William Williams by his same Will have devised and bequeathed the said premises to Chichester Wrey second son of the said Bourchier Wrey the Father and to the use of the said Chichester Wrey for and during the term of his natural Life without impeachment or Waste.

And after the Death of the said Chichester Wrey to Us our Heirs and Successors and to the use of us our Heirs and Successors for every subject nevertheless to the annual Rent and Incumbrances before mentioned as by the appointed Will more fully appears.

And the said Sir Wm Williams afterwards died without any Heirs of his Body lawfully begotten. And whereas after the Death of the said Sir Wm Williams to wit on an Inquisition indented taken at Carnarvon in the county of Carnarvon on the 25th day of October now last past before Thomas Price Esquire and others our Commissioners by Virtue of out commission under the Great Seal of England bearing Date of Westminster the 15th Day of August now last past to the said Commissioners and other Commissioners in the same Commission named or any Three or more of them directed upon the Oath of good and lawful men in the County of Carnarvon aforesaid it stands found that the aforesaid Sir Wm Williams in his Lifetime and at the Time of his Death was seized in his Dememsne as of Ffee of and in divers Manors Messuages Tenements Tofts Barns Stables Mills Structures Cottages Shops Lands Meadows Ffeedings pastures Rents and other Hereditament sin the said County of Carnarvon and of and in the several Reversions of Divers Messuages, Tenements Orchards Mills Lands Meadows pastures Rents and hereditaments in the said County of Carnarvon All and singular which Manors Messuages Tenements Tofts Barns Stables Mills Structures cottages Orchards Lands Meadows

Ffeedings pastures Rents and Hereditaments in the said Inquisition and also in these our Letters patent are more fully specified.

And by another Inquisition indented taken at Perthapthew in the said county of Anglesey the 28th Day of October now last past before Thomas Fletcher Edward Price and John Doulben our Commissioners by virtue of another our Commisssion under the Great Seal of England dated at Westminster on the 15th day of August now last past to the same Commissioners and others directed upon the Oath of good and lawful men of the county of Anglesey aforesaid it stands found that the said Sir Wim Williams in his Lifetime and at the time of his Death was seized on his Demesne of Ffee of and in divers Messuages Tenements Lands Rents and Hereditaments in the said County of Anglesey in the Inquisition last mentioned and also in these our Letters Patent more fully specified.

Now Know Ye that We of our special Grace and out of our certain knowledge and mere motion and also for divers good Causes and Considerations in this Respect moving Have given and granted and by these presents for ourselves our Heris and Successors Do give and grant unto our beloved and faithful subject John Gore Esquire his Heirs and assigns for ever our Reversion and Reversions Remainder and Remainders whatsoever expectant and depending upon the Estate and Interst for the Life of the said Bourchier Wrey the Son and the Estate and Interest for the Life of the said Chichester Wrey by the Will aforesaid given or bequeathed or upon any Estate or Estates for the Life or the Lives of the said Bourchier Wrey the son and Chichester Wrey or either of them.

[*The original of this document details all the land owned by the Faenol estate at the time*]

Notes and References

1. Penrhyn MSS 329-331.
2. This marriage took place before the seventeenth-century house called Plas Newydd was built, however there was undoubtedly a house there at this time which may have been called 'Betws y Glynne' (pers. comm. Dr Sheila Roberts, 2009).
3. This subject was discussed in some detail by T. Jones Pierce in the 1940 (vol 2) edition of the *Transactions of the Caernarfonshire Historical Society* (pp 38–47).
4. Jenkins, Geraint, *The Foundations of Modern Wales: Wales 1642–1780*, p 181, 1993.
5. Ibid, p 180, 1993.
6. Note that the chapel at Penrhyn Castle was moved to its present location as part of later changes. There are two good examples of seventeenth-century estate chapels in north Wales – one at Gwydir Uchaf outside Llanrwst and the other part of the Rhûg estate at Corwen.
7. Yates, W. N., Rûg Chapel, Llangar Church, Gwydir Uchaf Chapel, Cardiff, 2005.
8. Meaning 'Jane wife of the previous ...'
9. Ed E. G. Jones 'A description of Caernarfonshire (1809–1811)', Edmund Hyde Hall, *Caernarfonshire Historical Society Record Series No 2*, Caernarfon, 1952.
10. This is indeed a very separate part of the house – recent renovations discovered that the seventeenth-century builders had simply butted the extension up to the original building rather than keying the new stonework into the older walls. Cowboy builders are nothing new!
11. Copy of the will of Edward Williams of Maes-y-Castell, 16 Dec 1600, University of Wales Bangor (UWB), Baron Hill MS 2535.
12. See for example UWB, Baron Hill MSS 2716, 2717–28 & 2730–31.
13. UWB, Baron Hill MSS 2717–28.
14. UWB, Baron Hill MSS Calendar, vol 2, 1329–1752 Caernarfonshire, UWB, Baron Hill MSS 2631-2, original will of Henry Williams of Maes-y-Castell, 25 Dec 1658.
15. *Transactions of the Caernarfonshire Historical Society*, vol 28, p 24.
16. For further details see the Baron Hill index and documents held at the archives at UWB from the document numbers 2475 to well into the 2700s.
17. Additionally the chimney in this location facilitates the fireplace in the new kitchen in the basement below.
18. *Transactions of the Caernarfonshire Historical Society*, vol 49, p 161, 1988.
19. *Transactions of the Caernarfonshire Historical Society*, vol 49, p 172, 1988.
20. Calendar of Wynn (of Gwydir) papers 1515–1690, NLW, MS 1388, 1926.
21. Dodd, A. H., *Transactions of the Caernarfonshire Historical Society*, vol 28, pp 29–30.
22. Calendar of Wynn (of Gwydir) papers 1515–1690, NLW MSS 1411.
23. Calendar of Wynn (of Gwydir) papers 1515–1690, NLW MSS 1417.
24. Calendar of Wynn (of Gwydir) papers 1515–1690, NLW MSS 1420.

154 The Origins of the Faenol Estate

25. Tucker, N. *North Wales & Chester in the Civil War* (3rd edition), p 206, 2003.
26. Calendar of Wynn (of Gwydir) papers 1515–1690, NLW MS 1135.
27. See for example Baron Hill MSS 2611–13, 2615–6.
28. Carved in typical Arts and Crafts script on the underside of the door arch, Lady Sybil's inscription reads 'Ye mystic garden, fold me close, I love thee well, beloved Faenol'.
29. Pers comm., Reg Chambers Jones, 2007.
30. Montgomery Collection, vol 9, h357–64, the Anwyl Manuscript, NLW Brogyntyn MSS, re: Lewis Anwyl of Park.
31. A dower is a life estate to which a wife is entitled on the death of her husband – this might be land, property or goods.
32. UWB Baron Hill MS 3239, agreement between Sir Griffith Williams and Dame Margaret Williams.
33. The principal justice of the peace of a county, who is the keeper of the records of the county lit. 'Keeper of the Rolls'. A role given, according to one contemporary William Lambarde, author of various legal manuals, to a man for the most part especially picked out either for wisdom, countenance or credit. http://legal-dictionary.thefreedictionary.com/Custos+rotulorum & http://www.answers.com/topic/custos-rotulorum.
34. Also MP for Beaumaris 1597, 1604, 1614 and for Caernarfon in 1601. He died in the December after William and Margaret's wedding and was buried in Lincoln's Inn Chapel in London.
35. Now the site of the Market Hall on Palace Street.
36. Some examples of these receipt books were handed down for so many generations that they have reached the present day. One such was published by Hilary Spurling and she describes it as a 'small, stout, handwritten book, bound in leather and stamped in gold' which she inherited from a great aunt of her husband. The author was a Lady Elinor Fetiplace, a contemporary of Sir William William's parents. *Elinor Fetiplace's Receipt Book*, reprinted in 2008 (ISBN 9780571247332).
37. Tucker, N. *North Wales in the Civil War*, 1958.
38. Dodd, A. H., *A History of Caernarvonshire, 1284–1900*, p 196, 1968.
39. 1642 September 15. Derbye. King Charles I to the Commissioners of Array and Sheriff of Caernarvonshire. 'Whereas a rebellion has been raised and forces are marching against him, he [the King] is necessitated, for the defence of his own person and crown and the religion and law established, to will recipients to bring to the royal standard at Shrosburie the horse and foot of the Carnarvonshire trained bands, together with volunteers. If members of the trained bands cannot come, they are to send their sons, servants, or other volunteers in their places, together with their arms. It is intended that they, along with the trained bands and volunteers of other counties in the dominions of Wales, should form a regiment as a guard for the Prince; they will be received into the royal pay at Shrewsburye. Desires the county to furnish them with sufficient military supplies and stores for their journey, and money to bear their charge. Requires all JPs in the county to render assistance.' MSS Llanfair-Brynodol 35 (Howells, B.E., *A Calendar of Letters Relating to North Wales 1533–c.1700*, Cardiff, 1967).
40. 1642 October 29. Woodstocke. King Charles I to the Commissioners of Array of Caernarvonshire. 'Although letters have been sent to the recipients and several

persons who had collected the public money, ordering it to be paid to colonel John Owen towards the charge of the regiment he was appointed to raise, the King understands that no part of the money has been paid as directed, and that the regiment which was appointed to march immediately is in danger of disbanding from want of present supply. The payment of this money to the Colonel is of more service than if it had been sent direct to the writer, who would have sent it towards the supplying of that regiment: he desires still to have cause to continue his gracious opinion of his subjects of that county, being confident that if no satisfaction is given, it is through the coldness or disaffection of some particular persons who refer private ends before the public.' NLW Llanfair-Brynodol MSS 35 (Howells, B.E., *A Calendar of Letters Relating to North Wales 1533–c.1700*, Cardiff, 1967.

41. Tucker, from *Calendar of Wynn (of Gwydir) papers 1515–1690*, 1749.
42. Now Penrhyn Castle, at National Trust property in Llandegai, Bangor, Gwynedd.
43. Tucker, 2nd ed., op cit, pp 72, 95.
44. Tucker, 2nd ed., op cit, p 72.
45. Sequestration — confiscation of land and or property
46. Dodd, op cit, p 131,
47. Ibid, p 134.
48. Temporall state – worldly goods.
49. Will of Sir William Williams of Vaynol Caernarvonshire 1659: PRO B 11/291.
50. UWB Baron Hill MS 3239.
51. Calendar of Wynn (of Gwydir) papers 1515–1690, NLW MSS 2163.
51. UWB Baron Hill MS 3239.
52. Howells, B.E., *A Calendar of Letters Relating to North Wales 1533–c.1700*, p 18, Cardiff, 1967
53. NLW Mostyn MS 1343.
54. Williams, G.H. (1981) Farming in Stuart Caernarfonshire, *Transactions of the Caernarvonshire Historical Society*, vol 42, p 75, Caernarfon, 1981.
55. Richards, H.F., *The New Kalendars of Gwynedd*, Denbigh, 1994.
56. Henning, B. D. *History of Parliament: The Commons 1660–1690*. vol 3, Members M–Y, 1983. Warburg for the History of Parliament Trust, 736. In what sense Heneage Finch was his kinsman is not clear, or even which Heneage Finch it was. The two candidates are Sir Heneage Finch, 1st Earl of Nottingham, or perhaps more likely his son, the 1st Earl of Aylesford, who, like Sir William Williams, was a Tory MP (of William's father's generation). It is feasible to imagine from his biography how the two men might have met, but not how they might be termed 'kinsmen'. www.thepeerage.com/p2729.htm£i27289 accessed 08/01/08. The 3rd Earl of Aylesford, also Heneage Finch, did in fact have a link with Faenol through his daughter-in-law's sister who married Thomas Assheton Smith of Faenol around a hundred years later. This is of little help to this present quest.
57. *Sea Chart: the Menai Straits. Presented and dedicated to the Rt. Worshipfull Sir William Williams, Baronet*, by Capt G. Collins, 1696.
58. Cruikshanks, E. et al, *The History of Parliament: The House of Commons, 1690–1715*, p 873, Cambridge, 2002.
59. Thomas Bulkeley could have been the Thomas Bulkeley of Dinas who was at the same time his mother's brother and his wife's uncle (and also, as it happened the second husband of William's great-aunt Jane, née Griffith, of Castellmarch).

Alternatively, and more probably, he may have been the Thomas Bulkeley of William's own generation – his wife Elin's brother.
60. PRO, ref C66/3412
61. Eardley-Wilmot, Sir John E. *A Famous Fox-Hunter. Reminiscences of the Late Thomas Assheton Smith Esq or The Pursuits of an English Country Gentleman*, London, 1893.
62. *Journal of House of Commons 1693–1697*, vol 11, HC/CL/JO/2/13 and vol 12, HC/CL/JO/2/14.
63. National Library of Wales, Dictionary of Welsh Biography http://yba.llgc.org.uk/en/s-OWEN-BOD-1545.html accessed 07/07/2009.
64. *Journal of House of Commons 1693–1697*, vol 12, p 141.
65. Ibid, p 142.
66. Given that the Thomas Bulkeley of Dinas mentioned earlier was now 65 years of age, we might assume that this Bulkeley was the Thomas of the following generation. Although Thomas Bulkeley of Dinas lived to be 75, at 65 he might have felt himself a bit old for going out and menacing people.
67. *Journal of the House of Commons*, 1697, p 142.
68. At the beginning of Queen Anne's reign (1703) a pamphlet, *The Secret History of the Calves-Head Club; or, the Republican unmask'd*, was published. The author of the web site *The Book of Days* states that 'this tract appears to have excited the curiosity of the public in no small degree; for it passed, with many augmentations as valueless as the original trash, through no less than nine editions.' They quote a specimen of the verses quoted from the anthem for 1696, in reference to Charles I:

> This monarch wore a peaked beard,
> And seemed a doughty hero,
> A Dioclesian innocent,
> And merciful as Nero.
>
> The Church's darling implement,
> And scourge of all the people,
> He swore he'd make each mother's son
> Adore their idol steeple;
>
> But they, perceiving his designs,
> Grew plaguy shy and jealous,
> And timely chopt his calf's head off,
> And sent him to his fellows.

http://www.thebookofdays.com/months/jan/30.htm. Accessed 08/01/08
69. Tawstock near Barnstaple, Devon.
70. Andover, Hampshire.
71. Gwynedd Archives Service [GAS], Faenol Papers, MSS 4058 & 4059.
72. GAS, Faenol Papers, MS 2508.
73. Griffith, J. E., *Pedigrees of Anglesey & Carnarvonshire Families*, p 385: Lloyd of Pant & Gwyddfrynie, Llanegryn, Wrexham, 1985.
74. Griffith, J. E., *Pedigrees of Anglesey & Carnarvonshire Families*, p 368, the line of descent of the Smith/Assheton Smith/Duff family at Faenol.
75. Empress sized slates at 26" x 16", Kings at 36" x 20".

76. Faenol MS 2608.
77. Jones, J. (nd) *Hanes bywyd y diweddar Ellis James, Ty'n Llwyn, Bangor /A life history of the late Ellis James, Ty'n Llwyn, Bangor.* Reproduced by kind permission of Mr Struan James-Robertson.
78. Ibid.
79. Described in his obituary as 'not a popular preacher but a good one' http://www.rwgevans.com/family/web/family/pafg03.htm. Image of John Jones http://www.rwgevans.com/family/web/family/images/2600.jpg.
80. Roberts, p 63, 1973.
81. In 1872 Daniel Roberts built himself a new house not far away at Penrhosgarnedd, naming it Bryn Adda in recognition of the years he had spent at the farm. The house is now gone, but survives in the name of a cul-de-sac of houses built on the site.
82. Information courtesy of Miss Roma Lort Jones, 2009.
83. NLW Brogyntyn MSS, Montgomeryshire Collection, vol 9, h.357–64.
84. UWB Baron Hill MS 3232.
85. UWB Baron Hill MS 3247.
86. Patent Rolls, 21 March 1699, PRO C66/3413.

Index

A basic index to people, places and organisations mentioned in the body of the text.

Aberpwll	17
Allanson, Charles	84, 85, *85*, 89–90, 92, 93
Anwyl, Catherine	57
Anwyl, Lewis	57–8, 59
Babington Plot	16
Bangor	9, 12, 31, *31*, 58, 62, 68
Bangor, Hugh	17, 36, 86
Baron Hill, Beaumaris	40, 43, 44, 62, 80, 84, 85
Barrington, John	84, 88–9
Bartlett, Captain John	73
Bayley, Bishop Lewis	53
Beaumaris	54
Beeston Castle	64
Bodfel, Sir John	43
Bodysgallen	75, 76
Brereton, Colonel	64
Bryn Adda	99–100, 101
Bryn Iorkin (Hope)	77
Bryn Terfel	9
Bulkeley, Sir Richard	40
Bulkeley, Visct Robert	74, 80–1
Bulkeley, Thomas	62, 82, 90
Byron, Lord	64, 66
Caernarfon	9, 69
Caernarfon Castle	60, 66
Calves Head Club	90
Capel-y-Graig	55
Carr, Professor Tony	52
Carter, Colonel John	67
Castellmarch	60, *60*, 70, 73, 77
Cemaes	57
Chester	57, 64, 88
Clennenau	67
Cochwillan (Llandegai)	10, 12, *14*, *20*, 22, 25, 29, 36, 70, 96
Codcroft, Simon (cook)	70
Coed Helen (Caernarfon)	22
Conwy	36, 71
Court of Star Chamber	71
Cromwell, Oliver	67
Dafydd ap Llywelyn	45
Dalar Hir, Y	67
Davis, Dorothy	87–8
Davis, Thomas	92
de Haunton, William	23
Dinorwic, manor of	19, 29, 35, 53, 67, 80
Dodd, Professor A. H.,	
Duff, Robert	100
Ednyfed Fychan	10, 45
Eglwyseg	54
English Civil War	10, 59, 63–76
Evans, Ellen	84, 88
Evans, John (steward)	70, 84, 88–9, 90, 92
Evans, Hugh	90
Farchwell	17
Finch, Heneage	80
Felinheli, Y	17, 56
Fleet Prison	53
Frondeg	18
Gethin, Thomas	15
Gladstone, David	105
Glascoed Hall	96
Glynn, John	91, 92
Glynne, William (Plas Newydd)	18
Gore, John	83, 93
Griffith, Dean Edmund	43
Gruffith, William (Caernarfon)	60, 70
Gruffydd, Maurice	21
Gruffydd, Rowland	21
Gwydir Castle	22, *22*, 30, 40, 43, 54, 70
Hawarden Castle	64

Hall, Edmund Hyde	32	Plas Dinas (Llanwnda)	73
Hughes, Mr	92	Plas Dinorwic	56–7
Hughes, Betty (cook)	96–7	Plas Llanfair (Llanfairisgaer)	73
James, Catherine	97	Plas Mawr (Caernarfon)	60
James, Ellis	97–9, *97*, 100, 101	Plas Mawr (Conwy)	36, 37
James, Jane	97–8, *98*	Plas Newydd (Anglesey)	21, 96
Jenkins, Geraint (historian)	27	Plas Penmynydd (Anglesey)	25
Jones, Griffit	60, 66, 70, 77	Plas Newydd (Glynllifon)	18
Jones, Jane	60	Port Dinorwic	99
Jones, Revd John	99, *99*	Pryscol (Llanrug)	58, 72, 74
Jones, Robert	64	Ranulf, earl of Chester	45
Jones, Sir William (Castellmarch)	60	Reed, John	101
Jones, William (under-agent)	94	Rhos Einion	42
Kent, Benjamin	102	Rhos-y-Vengill,	42
Kent, Caroline	102	Roberts, Anne	99
Kent, James	102	Roberts, Daniel	99–100
Lewes ab Owen ap Meirick (Y Frondeg, Llangaffo)	18	Roberts, Edward	97–8
		St Mary Chapel (Faenol)	29–30, *30*, *37*, 56, 58
Lloyd, Eleanor	94	Salusbury, Dame Jane	85, 91
Lloyd, Morgan	94–5	Salusbury, Sir John	85
Lloyd, William	94	Smith, Sir Charles Assheton	29
Llanbeblig Church	60, *61*	Smith, John (Speaker)	83, 93, 94
Llandegai Church	*28*	Smith, George Duff Assheton	100, 102, 103
Llandegai	29, 62, 67		
Llandeiniolen	29	Smith, Henry	93
Llangadwaladr	30	Smith, Lady Sybil Assheton	56
Llangaffo	18	Smith, Thomas	93
Llanrug	58, 72	Smith, Bt, Sir Charles	104
Llywelyn Fawr, prince	10, 45	Smith, Thomas Assheton	94, 95, 96, 97, 100
Lort, William 'Beaver'	102–3, *102*		
Maenol Bangor	17	Stanley, Edward, earl of Derby	16
Maes-y-Bont	17	Stanley, Jane	16–18, 31–2
Maes-y-Castell	40, *41*, *42*, 43	Stanley, Roland	16, 17
Melai	68	Stanley, Sir William	16
Meyrick family (Bodorgan)	85	Tawstock	93
Morgan, Hugh	90, 91	Tedworth (Hampshire)	83, 94
Morgan, Richard	12–15	Thirty Years War	59
Mostyn, Sir Roger	50, 53, 74	Thomas, John (undercook)	70
Myddleton, Colonel	64	Thomas, Sir William (Coed Helen)	53
Mytton, General	66, 67	Thomas Wyn ap Wilim	12–32, 47, 78, 96
Owen, MP, Arthur	84, 85, 86–90, 91–2		
Owen, Major-General Sir John	67, 73	Trafford, Thomas	54
Pandora (steam yacht)	103	Tucker, Norman	64
Parry, John	88, 91–2	Tŷ Gwyn (Llanberis)	98
Penmaenmawr	58	Ty'n Llwyn (Pentir)	101
Penrhyn	10, 12, 22, 62, 64, 96	Wexford, Ireland	73
Plas Coch (Anglesey)	25		

White, William 85, 87
Wîg (Abergwyngregyn) 50, 54
William Wyn ap Wilim 12
Williams, Lady Dorothy 36, 37–8, 40–4, 49, 52, 75
Williams, Edward (Maes-y-Castell) 40, 42
Williams, Edward (Wîg) 50
Williams, Edward 88
Williams, Elen 18
Williams, Lady Ellen (née Bukeley) 80, 82, 84, 85, 86, 88
Williams, Elin 36–7, 49
Williams, Elinor 38
Williams, Elizabeth 50
Williams, 4th Bt, Sir Griffith 68, 70, 71, 72–7, 78
Williams, Henry 42–3, 54
Williams, Jane 54
Williams, Archbishop John 62, 64, *65*, 66, 67
Williams, Lady Katherine 18, 50, 54–5, 56, 57, 58, 72
Williams, Magdalen 56
Williams, Margaret 38
Williams, Lady Margaret (née Jones) 60–1, 68
Williams, Lady Margaret (née Wynn) 68–9, 70, 74
Williams, Lady Penelope (née Bulkeley) 74–5, 76, 78

Williams, Rache; (Ray) 105
Williams, Simon 18, 32, 54
Williams, Thomas (see Thomas Wyn ap Wilim)
Williams, Thomas 73
Williams, 2nd Bt, Sir Thomas 49, 50–9
Williams, 5th Bt, Sir Thomas 76
Williams, 1st Bt, Sir William 18, 32, 35–49, 53, 75
Williams, 3rd Bt, Sir William 59–72
Williams, 6th Bt, Sir William 76–84, *79, 80*, 85, 86, 91–2, 93
Willis, Browne 31
Wrey, Sir Bourchier 82, 84, 85, 88, 91, 93
Wynn, Cadwaladar 90
Wynn, Colonel Hugh 76, *76*, 77, 80
Wynn, John (Melai) 70
Wynn, Bt, Sir John (Gwydir) 21, 52, 54, 71
Wynn, Owen 53, 54
Wynn, Sir Richard 30
Wynn, Richard 71
Wynn, Robert (Plas Mawr) 36, 37, 50, 51
Wynne, William 87, 89, 92
Yonge, Ellis 76